Relatable Stories of Life, Love, and Unexpected Journeys

Jean Walton
& Jaime Obertubbesing

ISBN: 979-8-9884426-2-2 (Paperback)
ISBN: 979-8-9884426-3-9 (Electronic)

First printing, 2024.

Missfit Press
Colorado Springs, CO

www.missfitpress.com

Adventure Accolades

"The stories are really great and funny!! I liked the honesty. And you wrote the stories with simplicity. It is a great book!"
~ C

"I enjoyed reading this compilation of everyday stories. It's like you're just sitting down with a friend, listening to them share with you their adventure or passion or something that's important to them. Some things relatable and others inspirational. Fun, short, easy, read."
~ Alicia McCarley

"I really enjoyed these wonderful stories by amazing women. Really enjoyed this book. I highly recommend"
~ Terra Garza

I'd like to dedicate this book to my brother, Michael, for inspiring me to write my first story.

Your story matters and reminded me that we all do. It gave me the courage to do things I never thought possible.

Thank you for showing me how to smile through all the good and bad moments.

~Jean

Acknowledgements

To all my sisters–I want to thank you for inspiring me, supporting me and coming along on these incredible adventures. I couldn't have done it without you.

Sisters– Mary, Christy, Margie, and Kelly

Everyday Girls–

Jaime	Shalesa	Susan
Reese	Kam	Mandy
Maggie	Sheridan	Jeri
Teresa	Carissa	Brenda
Shauna "the Fox"	Maritza	LaDreeva
Sarra	Sunnie	Rebecca
Traci	Maria	Erika
Romi	Kate	Alicia
Jamie	Tabby	Cynthia
Holly	Stephanie	Rachael
Charlene	Kimberly	Alisha
Nino	Carrin	Michelle
Tonia	Lorine	April
Rachel	Wanda	Stacy
	Kay	Jennifer

And so many more....If you haven't yet made it into the pages of an *Everyday Adventures* book, stay tuned. These adventures are just getting started.

Adventure Atlas

Preface...1

Destination 1:
Everyday Family Adventures:

Jean Walton– 'Miss'ellaneous Sister Adventures.............................5
Kate Thierry– Calling in Manifestation Magic..............................22
Wanda Ortiz– A Road Trip to a New Beginning...........................29
Jasmine Rasch– A Man of Joy...36

Destination 2:
Everyday Love Adventures

Magnus Downs– Breaking the Damn Dam....................................44
Reese Walton– 'Miss' Me More..60
Tabby Halsrud– How a Couple of Misfits Found Love: How a
  Miss Found Her Mister...68
Garrett Goggans–How a Couple of Misfits Found Love: How a
  Mister Found His Miss..80

Destination 3:
Everyday Career Adventures

Jaime Obertubbesing– 'Miss'chevious Adventures in Retail........89
Susan Kilrain– Slaying Snakes in the Cockpit..............................105
Mike Meyers– Life Through Basketball...116

Shalesa Aldrich– 'Miss'guided Career Paths................................124

Ashley Anderson– Three Generations of Small Business
    Ownership...130

William Baxter– Noble Cause Adventures in the Workforce.....136

Destination 4:
Everyday Travel Adventures

Kelly Calabrese– Adventures of the Galapagos Hopper.............146

Bill Stanley– I Was a Stowaway in the Solomon Islands.............153

Sunnie LaMarre– How High is Too High?................................161

Destination 5:
Everyday Pet Adventures

Kay Rowe– My Bestie Pets...173

Cuzco, the Dog– Driving to Alaska: Why the Dog Had the
    Most Fun..183

Preface

Adventure is everywhere. It's in the simple events of day-to-day life; in the Sunday afternoons we spend with our families; in the mishaps and learning curves at work; in the spontaneous day trips or vacations to a new destination; and in the reconnections with friends, old and new. It's in the hard decisions to change careers and follow a dream; in the chances we take on just an idea; and even in the small quiet moments we experience when no one is watching. The point is, you don't have to lead an extravagant life to find extraordinary moments. You just have to be willing to look for them.

Over the years, I realized that my favorite adventures are found in the memories made with the people I love. Whether it be a girl's trip to a fun destination, checking out the latest venue in town, falling asleep watching movies on the couch, or simply a meaningful conversation over coffee (or wine), I count *my* blessings in these everyday moments. For me, it's not about what I'm doing, but who I am spending it with.

And that's exactly what *Everyday Adventures* is—finding the magic in even the smallest of moments. It's a chance for people from all walks of life to share their sense of adventure in the big, small, and inspirational moments of their everyday lives. Our hope is that you will be inspired to view every single day as a new opportunity to make your own amazing memories.

Remember, it is ultimately up to each of us to decide what to do with the moments we are given. And we experience thousands of new ones every day. Why not choose to find the best in even the worst of situations, and allow our adventures to teach us, mold us, and give us something to smile about? So, wear the dress. Doordash the chocolate cake. Plan the vacation. Take the leap of faith. Put your dreams into motion. We only have one life—why not make it worth remembering?

XOXO Jaime

'Miss'-cellaneous Sister Adventures

By Jean Walton

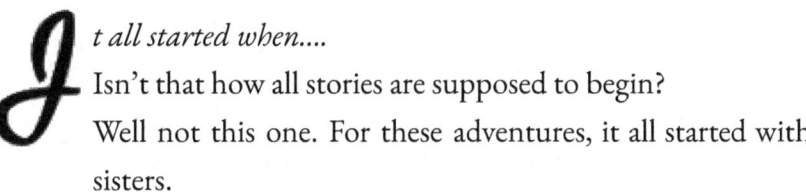

t all started when....
Isn't that how all stories are supposed to begin?
Well not this one. For these adventures, it all started with sisters.

I have four sisters. Two older and two younger. I'm right in the middle. I also have five brothers, but this story is all about the girl-time.

When I was younger, I idolized the older ones, Mary and Christy. They were in a band, and always had the most fun. And they wore the kind of clothes I wished I could wear, but I had neither the curves nor the maturity yet.

I was closest with my younger sisters, Margie and Kelly, growing up. Most of my siblings are roughly two years apart. But I was the oldest of the younger set, so the three of us were grouped together. Everyone always referred to us as "the girls".

We didn't always get along–the normal squabble-every-now-and-again family. The hair pulling days and fighting throughout our childhood aren't exactly the fondest of memories, but a very normal part of growing up in a large family. However, disagreements never lasted long. There's something about family that makes you resilient to get over the drama. At least more easily when a bad day meant missing out on a second bowl of cereal or not being able to find your favorite shirt you wanted to wear to school that day.

My earliest sister memory is when I buried Margie's sandals in the sandbox. I was three or four. When it was time to go home, Christy helped me dig and search, but with no success. We had to carry two ish-year-old Margie back to our apartment. I still giggle sheepishly when I retell that story. And also, I wonder what happened to those dang sandals!

I didn't really have much of a friend group growing up. I was extremely shy and often bullied in school, so I kept to myself. Instead, I considered my sisters to be my friends. Especially Margie–she was my best friend.

Margie and I were often mistaken for twins. We didn't really look alike, but our similar mannerisms and voices fooled people. My mom also dressed us in the same outfits, just in different colors. We were practically inseparable–playing with dolls when we were home, going to the playground, and riding bicycles in the neighborhood. If I did something, Margie did too. If she did, sometimes I would. I could be kind of a scaredy cat at times.

"Don't ask for anything!" my mom would say at the store. As the quintessential rule follower, I was the only one who would listen. I didn't like negative consequences, so if I was told not to do something, I didn't do it. I stayed silent. Yet, somehow when we were leaving, Margie and Kelly would always manage to walk out with candy and a pop, while I left empty handed. My mom would say, "You didn't ask for anything," when I would complain. "I did what I was told," I replied.

When I was eight, my parents decided to form a family band called 'Family Affair' with my older siblings. I was too young to be in the band, but I could sing, so I would perform for schoolmates and their parents. I usually got picked for solos at the Christmas pageants too. However, the first time I sang on a microphone in front of my class, I heard, "She sounded way better NOT on the microphone," from a boy in my class as I was walking off the stage. It shattered my confidence forever, and I had a hard time getting up to sing in front of people after that.

My shyness got worse, but my FOMO did not. I loved watching my family perform, and my sisters and I were happy to get up and sing whenever we were allowed. I always joke that I grew up in bars, but I sort of did. Despite being underage, my older siblings were permitted to go into bars to play a gig. By default, Margie, Kelly, and I were too. What a unique education a young girl gets that way! Oh, nothing too inappropriate, of course–mostly just embarrassment when trying to order our own piña coladas at the bar, not knowing that previously when other people ordered them for us they were mocktails. I can still hear those laughs from the patrons around us and remember my hot face.

In a large family, solitude is a rarity and you don't truly experience anything alone. You're first, last or in the middle when it comes to life's lessons. And comparison is inevitable. Someone is always best, worst or mediocre. I often felt I was the latter of the three when I was compared to my sisters, no matter who was the first to do things.

That never bothered me for too long though. My adoration for my sisters has always outweighed any bitterness or jealousy. To this day, I still love cheering them on and seeing them perform, even though I don't have a lot of confidence in my own singing abilities anymore.

As we became young women, I had to accept that my dreams of becoming a famous singer would never be fulfilled. It was time for other adventures. At the age of 16, I started working as a waitress, first at Perkins, then at various restaurants on and off over the course of 10 years. Italian, Mexican, Cajun–despite this international cuisine education, it was not exactly a life dream. And because I was shy, my customer service skills weren't that great at first either. But as with anything, if you keep putting yourself out there, you get used to it and find a way to make it work.

I met Michelle at the Italian restaurant, Carini's. She was sure of herself and everything she did, including waitressing. I looked up to her like I did my sisters and followed her lead. Not long after we became close, she gave me a week to decide if I was going to move to Seattle with her the following month. I was 22 and spontaneous, so I thought, "What the heck!"

Well, 'poor in the city' was an adventure, that's for sure. A month's worth of savings as a waitress doesn't get you too far. But somehow, we managed to tough it out and get through those first few months. We started new waitressing jobs at a Mexican restaurant called Azteca and lived on free chips and salsa lunches to get by.

After acclimating ourselves, Michelle invited her friend, April, to join our 'girls in the city' adventures. Things were finally starting to get fun and a lot less tight when I managed to get myself pregnant. Although I did everything I could to make my relationship work, I was not in love, so those were some of the most lonely and down moments for me as a new mom. I had my beautiful baby boy to take care of. So, I took refuge with my sister, Mary, who generously let me move in with her, and went back home to good old Rapid City, SD, to raise my baby on my own.

Something about sisters–they're always there waiting on the sidelines when you need them, no matter what.

From that point on, I worked on regaining my independence. I eventually got married and settled into a military family lifestyle, with three kids, two boys and a girl. Living a military life means that you must pick up and be ready to start over every four years or so. When we moved to Florida and then England, I missed my family terribly and traveled back as often as possible. But

I managed to create a close-knit friend group every place I've lived to fill the void.

Girlfriends are another form of sisterhood that I treasure. I've been fortunate enough to form some really strong bonds over the years.

When my family and I relocated to Florida on our first duty station move, I had to leave my sisters behind. But I quickly connected with my new friend, Jamie. We met at the park while our kids played together. It's so easy for kids to ask each other to play, and then before you know it they're best friends. It's not as effortless as we get older, but somehow that's exactly what my friendship was like with Jamie. The adventures in those days revolved around chatting away at the park, going to movies, or spending five hours at the mall trying on clothes for our girls-night-out dancing weekends. Those are fond memories to me. It felt just like having another sister around.

But alas, after the four years were complete, it was time to move again. Off to jolly ol' England we went. Following my kids' lead, I was able to make some girlfriends right away despite living off base in the small village of Red Lodge. The villages are pretty small in England, so most of my friends lived in different ones 20 to 30 minutes away from me. Almost everything was that close of a drive. Except for London–that was a two hour commute. But some of the other "cities" were closer by. Newmarket, where horse races occur regularly, was only a 15 minute drive from my village, and one of my favorite places to meet up with friends for a girl's day. I didn't mind waiting on the majestic creatures, led by their jockeys, as they crossed the road and backed up traffic. However, I did have quite the culture shock with having to drive on the wrong side of the road. And those round-a-bouts—they were everywhere! Talk about added anxiety. (Thank goodness I'm not prone to road rage!) But those friends, who once again became my new family, made things smooth enough for England to truly feel like home too.

I caught the travel bug immediately after my first European trip to Amsterdam. My sister, Christy, was touring the Netherlands with her husband, so my husband and I asked another couple to watch our kids for the weekend, and we met up with them for a Dutch adventure! Amsterdam has a lot of beautiful canals and museums everywhere you turn. Fall in Europe is especially a feast for the eyes. All the colors are enchantingly vibrant, and there's so much amazing culture to immerse yourself in. A stroll through the red-light district was *interesting* to say the least.

I had quite a few adventures over the years with Christy. Since London was only two hours away from my village, I became a pro at navigating the tube (London's version of a subway) to meet up with her for spontaneous day trips when she traveled there for work. But, no matter where I've lived, we have made a point to continue our sister travels back to London, Paris, Portugal, and even

Italy! Touring Italy's iconic cobblestone streets, flooded with fountains and majestic cathedrals, is an all-time favorite of mine.

Exploring castles is one of my most treasured experiences. I loved taking my kids to ancient castle grounds and making memories as a family when they were young. To say they were less than thrilled is an understatement, as they grumbled and complained at the very suggestion. But as for my sisters, girlfriends, and I—we still jump up and down at the chance to explore! Traveling and discovering new places never gets old. It is even more special as a sisterhood adventure.

It was so easy and affordable to hop from country to country during my time in England. My friends and I loved taking weekend girl's getaways as often as possible. My first trip to Paris with Tonia was in the dead of winter on the coldest possible weekend we could have chosen to go. But a snowstorm didn't put a damper on our spirits. Some of those miserably cold moments just added to the stories. Deciding to have fun no matter what, we bundled up and trekked out onto the beautiful French streets, basking in the wonder of it all. We had each other to share the adventures, and the memories made it all worth the cold hands, feet, and red noses.

Spain, Portugal, Italy, Belgium, and Greece—we wanted to experience it all. And for some reason the most dramatic occurrences happened whenever Tonia and I were traveling together. I think we got lost at some point in each destination. Portugal was especially concerning as we worried for our lives with our crazy taxi driver who didn't seem to know what stop signs were for. Our decision to go out dancing the first night was ill advised when we got locked in a bar during a terrible windstorm. Since our hotel was a few blocks away, they barred the doors, forcing us to stay inside for our safety. I danced for six hours straight to pass the time (quite the workout!), while Tonia learned to juggle bottles of liquor, much like Tom Cruise in the movie, *Cocktail*. But their decision to hold us captive seemed legit as we were walking home the next morning amongst all the downed trees. After some much needed shut-eye, we dared to venture out once again and got lost in the rain on the next quest for fun and memory making.

I'll never forget the time we celebrated my birthday in Corfu, Greece. On the shuttle from the airport, we saw all the other people get excited as they were dropped off little by little at their fancy resorts. However, we were unimpressed, and mocked their enthusiasm between ourselves, as we were headed to a cute little hidden gem at the edge of the water, and couldn't help but think that our destination would prove to be more impressive.

Much to our surprise, we were dropped off late at night, in the middle of nowhere, left to our own devices next to an ominous and dark alley. The driver explained that our "hotel" was just down the path at the end. Skeptically, we walked into the dark abyss until we made our way to the ocean and somehow actually arrived at the inn, whose brick pathway was the only thing that even remotely resembled the pictures we had seen online. "We were waiting up for you!" greeted the friendly inn keeper and his wife, who then took our passports at check in and, to our astonishment, disposed of a lizard running rampant in our room. It was then decided to find one of those "fancy" resorts with proper amenities to stay at instead. The next morning we marched into the lobby and demanded our passports back. The innkeeper was not there, so his wife gave us cookies to smooth things over while we waited for his return. It was gracious of him to give us a ride to the nearest bus stop, though he did question whether or not we would give him a bad review.

I wish I could say it was smooth sailing from there, but we then had to navigate a bus system in a foreign country with lots of luggage and not a lot of English-speaking locals. Never mind the eternal hike up an unknown path that finally took us to our long-awaited oasis. But it was all worth it, as heaven's gates seemed to open right before us at the top of that hill. We were immediately served lemonades at check in and our mound of luggage magically whisked away to our suite. Bananas and wine awaited at our bedside, and I had never been to a hotel that gave you a personalized card and birthday cake before. The entire experience was right out of a dream.

The need to travel and explore did not end when I returned to live in the states. And since I am fortunate to have so many sisters now, I am able to enjoy frequent girl's trips throughout the year.

Europe is still a preferred destination of mine. The magic of being taken back in time is beyond anything I can describe.

A sister trip for Margie's 40th birthday was one for the books. The entourage included me, Margie, Christy and Margie's best friend, Shauna (who is now coined our "Italian sister"). We planned a 10-day tour through Italy's most renowned cities. Rome was first. I had been there once before with my ex-husband on one of his work trips, but much of that experience was spent with me meandering alone. Rome is so grand and majestic, you just can't help but wonder about all of the famously historic happenings that occurred and the people that walked those same cobblestone paths we get to today. Side note...if you ever go to Rome, please do yourself a favor and wear the most comfortable shoes that you have. I can't stress this enough. Crying in pain in the new boots I just *had* to have as I walked through the epic halls of the Vatican really took away from experiencing the amazing works of art and rich history. Thankfully, I had a do-over when I went again with my sisters and, just as importantly, some very comfortable footwear.

Something my sisters and I enjoy doing on a trip is finding matching hats to make the occasion a little more special. At first, we thought colored fedoras seemed appropriate to commemorate Italy. Plus it rains a lot, so we needed protection from the elements. A souvenir store in the midst of our wandering provided a few silly options for photo ops. We didn't expect the knitted baseball style hats with furry puffs on the top to be so flattering. As an added bonus, they came in four different colors–it seemed meant to be! And that's how we became "The Puff Squad", bonding our sisterhood forever.

I have also been blessed to explore some American cities that I'd never been to. I even took an international road trip with Christy and our friend, Sarra, from Boston all the way to Canada, making only two quick pit stops in New Hampshire–one for a classic photo op amongst the colorful foliage, and the other to stock up at one of their infamous cheap liquor stores. I loved every second of that expedition. With the cobblestone roads and city gates of Quebec, it felt just like being in France again!

Two trips will forever stand out in my mind as the ultimate sister adventures. The first was assisting Christy's epic, days-long, space gala extravaganza in London. I had the opportunity to be an assistant producer and work together with a team of incredibly talented women on a meaningful project. Christy works with astronauts and brought 11 of them to London to celebrate their achievements. As her assistant, I was tasked with organizing seating, delegating the volunteers, and checking in guests. Despite the stressful moments, it was rewarding to be part of such a special event to honor these iconic individuals. This is where I learned that no matter who you are, working hard together to make something special happen can truly bond you, especially as women. Not to mention, the spontaneous decision to jet off to Portugal and Jersey Island for some epic downtime after all the work was over was truly the cherry on the cake. But the best part was capturing the moments of singing, dancing, and laughing in pictures and videos that we can revisit time and time again to reminisce those moments over and over.

The other was when my best friend, Jaime, and I went to New York City to celebrate writing and publishing our very first book. Our collaboration had 16 different authors whom we brought together to share relatable, fun, and inspiring stories in the *Everyday Girl Adventures* book, one of my favorite "sister" projects. I had seen other authors and publishers promote their books on the bright billboards of Times Square, so we put together a video of all the authors to showcase on the Jumbotron. It was important to me to share this accomplishment with all of us, because that's the best way to appreciate a moment—when you have others to celebrate life with. I wanted to make this special experience happen. And I did. WE DID.

It wasn't the most glamorous of trips I've ever been on. We stayed in the POD hotel, which owned up to its name with the tiniest excuse for a hotel room you could ever imagine. A closet sized space (and I don't mean a walk-in), complete with bunk beds you had to shimmy around to even get to the bathroom, never mind squeezing in our luggage. However, it was surprisingly upscale and just a few blocks from Times Square. Needless to say, a 5-star review! It was also in the middle of December and rained practically the entire time. (No, we did not plan ahead and bring umbrellas as any experienced traveler would know to do.) We looked like drowned rats in most of the pictures we took–not exactly what I would have hoped for in our big Times Square debut. But nothing beats ice skating in Central Park during Christmas time, and the magic of this big moment was still there all the same.

Through all of these adventures, I realized something–no matter if you are sisters, friends, mothers or daughters, it isn't about being the best or the worst; it's about being together, making memories, and cherishing the bond we share. And that is how our story will always continue—with laughter, adventure, and the unbreakable bond of sisterhood.

Jean Walton

When Jean found herself starting over in life, divorced after a 17-year marriage, with 3 grown kids and a day job that lost its luster, she knew she needed something more. She has always looked for adventure in the smallest moments but realized that the true joy came from sharing those experiences with people around her.

Everyday Girl Adventures was born from just that. Jean's brand seeks and organizes fun and unique opportunities to bring people together and create lasting memories. Her goal is to help others recognize the joy of a moment and inspire them to find the adventure in their everyday life.

Jean also understands the value of women supporting women. As a misfit in the business world, she wanted to create a place where entrepreneurs of all backgrounds could feel empowered coming together, no matter the stage of their business. MissFit Networking Group is a place for just that—it's where every "miss" fits.

Jean's flair for adventure and passion for life are no secret to those who meet her. So how does she find adventure in her every day? The answer is simple: she says yes to every opportunity. She would rather take a risk than always wonder what could have been. You only live once—and ultimately, it's the memories, no matter how big or small, that make it all worth living.

✦ Calling in Manifesting Magic ✦

By Kate Thierry

J didn't grow up in what you would call a stable childhood. And the parenting I did receive was far from ideal. Actually, the way I often describe it, is that in many ways, I raised myself. In doing that, intuition was my strongest teacher and guide. It's something I now playfully call, "Kate Magic". It was born out of necessity, but has turned into one of my superpowers.

How this magic often shows up in my life is through manifestation. And I'd love to share a story with you about how I began working with manifestation consciously. It's the story of how my boys and I manifested a beautiful home using some of that magic!

I was married at the time, and we were living in a small, two bedroom apartment - less than 1,000 SF. My three boys were ages 8, 10, and 13. Not only that, but we also had a large dog and a full drum kit that we squeezed into that tiny space. To say that we were crammed in there is putting it lightly. Back then, money was really tight, and my boys were complaining about sharing a bedroom and needing more space–rightly so. I assured them that we would look for a house to rent when our lease was up that summer. However, looking at our financial situation, it became clear that renting a house would have to be put on the back burner, as putting money towards credit card debt needed to be our top priority.

As you can imagine, sharing this reality with the boys did not go over too well! Trying to reassure them, I explained that just because we needed to put money towards debt, didn't mean we couldn't *still* get a house. "How is that possible?" they protested. I told them that I really didn't know but that I believed anything's possible! They all rolled their eyes at me, but they had faith in their mama. All I knew was that this situation needed some intention, some hope, and a little magic!

I had often found myself winging things - engaging with the realm of possibility and intuition, simply because, so much of the time, it felt like I had nothing else. Years before, someone once told me, "If anyone can do it, you can!" And that became my inspiration and my motto. The Henry Ford quote, "Whether you believe you can do a thing or not, you are right," fueled my motivation, optimism, and adventures. This being the voice in my head, I recalled, and was inspired by, the magical events in Elizabeth Gilbert's book, *Eat, Pray, Love,* (chapters 91 & 92), where Tutti, a little girl in Bali, manifested a house for her and her mom. This in mind, I figured we needed a little manifestation magic to help us out. So, I got busy with the task of creating some of that magic with my boys!

I created a plan to sit together as a family, every weekend, visualizing the house we dreamed of living in. Now, this was a new experience for my boys. I'd never guided them through meditation before. And they weren't 100% onboard with all of mom's woo-woo, new age stuff. Fortunately, they weren't old enough to *completely* rebel against it, either. Now keep in mind, this was all happening before the practice of manifestation had become popular, and truth be told, I really didn't know what I was doing. I just wanted my boys to have hope. They definitely deserved it. And if anyone could do that for them, I could - right?!

I got the whole family gathered together in the living room, and I guided them through a visualization of the house they fantasized living in–How big was it? What did their bedroom look like? etc. But mostly, how did they *feel* being in their dream house? How did it *feel* to have a room of their very own? Fueled by the innocence, creativity, and excitement of my boys, it turned out to be a really rewarding experience. Afterwards, they shared their visualizations. They were mostly comprised of space–space of their own, and space to play!

Despite my original plan, I think we only ended up doing that activity once before my little concocted experiment fell off. But what I didn't know then, that I know now, is that letting go of any attachment to your desires is part of the manifestation practice. And apparently, that one time we visualized together is all it took for the magic to take hold!

Cut to a couple months later–I got a phone call from my youngest son's friend's mom. She said that my son had let her know that we were looking to rent a house. I explained that unfortunately, we really didn't have the money at the time. I had been in her big, beautiful home, and I knew it was far out of our price range. But she asked me to discuss the situation over lunch. She then explained that her family was going to be out of the country for a few years due to work. She shared that it would help them feel more at ease to know who was living in their home while they were away. In exchange for house and lawn maintenance, she offered us to rent their home, for only $150 more than what we were paying for our tiny apartment. And so, with an abundance of awe and wonder, of course, I gratefully accepted!

I remember checking out the house with my boys for the very first time. Mostly, I recall how it felt. It was surreal–knowing that this beautiful house was actually going to be our home. It definitely felt like magic. How did this happen? It was perfect–this two story, four bedroom, four bath, 2,300 SF home. It had an open floor plan, a finished basement, two fireplaces, and heated kitchen floors. The front yard was fully landscaped with a fountain, and the large backyard had a privacy fence with a deck coming off the living room/kitchen area. The owners even agreed to let me plant a veggie garden in the back!

I loved seeing the excitement in each of my boys as they explored their new space, claiming their very own bedrooms. My oldest son got the basement bedroom and my two younger boys were upstairs next to the master suite. One statement really sticks out in my memory from that day. It's that of my middle son excitedly proclaiming, "Mom, it's exactly how I pictured it!" That's when it truly hit me, just how magical this experience was. We had manifested that house!

Over those three years, our family had so many adventures in that beautiful home. And during that time I started learning more about manifesting, and eventually created my first vision board. Many things have been added to it over the years, and many have come to fruition. One of the first things that comes to mind is braces for my oldest son. We didn't have the means to get those sorely needed braces for him, so again, with no ideas of how to actually make it happen, only faith, we photoshopped a picture of him with braces onto my vision board. I don't even remember exactly how it came to be, but six months later, guess who had braces?! You bet he did!

That was almost two decades ago. My boys are all grown men now, and they each have their own, unique relationship with manifesting and magic making. Looking back, not only was living in that home a gift, but maybe the even bigger gift was the invaluable experience of showing my boys that magic does exist–that *they* are magic, and that anything truly *is* possible! And oh, has that been the experience over the years. At times they've each chosen to make and use their own vision boards. And they've uniquely created all kinds of magic in their lives. Collectively, they've manifested all sorts of experiences including: studying abroad, travel, jobs, relationships, amazing opportunities, and so much more.

As for me, I've continued growing my connection to my intuition and my "Kate Magic". It's at the forefront of who I am and at everything I do. Intuition and magic is something we all have and can tap into! I encourage you to find your own magic too.

Kate Thierry

I am a divorced mom of three grown young men; a passionate, creative, and powerful manifester; intuitive; yogi; dancer; healer; lifelong learner; lover of orchids and all things dark chocolate. I've had more than my share of adventures in this lifetime, but I'm not done yet!

These days you can find me enjoying life through the lens of the senses, prioritizing self-care and play, while living my purpose of facilitating safety, healing, and hope in the world.

A Road Trip to a New Beginning

By Wanda Ortiz

*I*t was Spring of 2018, and everything seemed to be going well in my life. I had been renting a four bedroom home shared with my three kids and boyfriend for three years. My oldest daughter had just recently moved out, and I had a whole living area downstairs, open to many possibilities.

I was working part-time jobs and looking for a more steady occupation to provide for my family. I decided to turn the basement into a daycare and become a home daycare provider in Fall of 2016. However, I was starting to feel a little bit of cabin fever with the cold weather and snow days in Colorado. I needed sunshine and water in my life, but a trip to Puerto Rico wasn't possible with time and expenses. I started searching for warm places nearby that I could get away for the weekend–not necessarily a beach–I would even be content with a pool.

Arizona quickly came to mind. My niece was living in Tucson at the time, and we hadn't seen her in a couple of years. I thought it would be nice to visit and for all of us to catch up.

Funny thing was that I chose not to mention this to my brother, my parents, or strangely enough, my niece. I calculated the 12 hour drive time and how many days we would need to stay in a hotel. I had to be back by 6 a.m., Monday morning, to receive the first child at my new daycare. There was also tension at home between my boyfriend and I, and I needed some time away. After confirming that his work schedule would not allow him to take time off, I decided to do a road trip alone with my kids.

This was going to be my first solo road trip. It was a little stressful with less than a few days to prepare. Not to mention, the negative talk I had received from my boyfriend and ex-husband put self-doubt in my head that I wasn't going to follow through and painted the idea that I couldn't do it on my own. Well, that just fueled my fire to prove them wrong.

Friday came and I had thrown together a cooler with snacks for everyone and laid down the back seats of my car for the kids to sleep in with pillows and blankets. All I had to rely on was my phone for directions. I booked a hotel with a pool, within the Tucson area, close to a military base. During this time, I was also actively serving in the Colorado Army National Guard. My backup plan was that my ID would allow me on base if my impromptu idea of meeting up with my niece fell through.

The trip didn't start off on schedule. Plans were originally to do most of the driving during daylight, but we didn't leave home until 7 p.m. My daughters were 19 and 16, so I knew I could rely on them to take the wheel if needed. I had my time precisely calculated, and my funds were tight. I was determined to drive straight through with minimal stops for food, bathroom breaks, and gas fill-ups.

My oldest daughter, Nishia, took the first portion of the drive. Ashley and Vincent were sleeping in the back, and we hardly had any traffic on the road. Things were going smoothly, until Nishia noticed that it was difficult for her to see on the county road. She started to flicker between the dash lights and high beams, and we quickly noticed one of the headlights had gone out. Unfortunately, so did the state patrol. We had just passed over the Colorado border into New Mexico. Right away I knew in my gut he was pulling us over. Of course we all panicked. Against my better judgment, I had chosen not to pack my son's booster seat to make room for the other items we were taking. The patrol officer noticed right away. He issued a warning for my lights but gave me a ticket for no seat for my six-year-old son. We quickly found the nearest Walmart in New Mexico to buy one. I did not let that damper my spirits and continued with our drive.

We would take turns driving between the three of us, for 30 minutes to an hour, to give our eyes a rest. When my kids were sleeping, I found myself alone in my thoughts. I got lost thinking about my current relationship and my career, questioning my happiness and feeling a void.

We finally made it to Tucson around 8 a.m. Exhausted and ready to lay on comfy beds, we discovered it was too early to check into the hotel. There was an IHOP next door, so we decided to eat there and call my parents to obtain my niece, Jasmine's, phone number. (I laugh now, but that was clearly poor planning on my part.) My parents were also very surprised to find out I'd gone on this trip alone. There I was, in an unfamiliar town, but determined to give my kids a nice spring break. Fortunately, we got a hold of Jasmine and coordinated to pick her up the next day to go to a nearby water park.

Finally, we were able to check into the hotel, and we all took a much needed nap. After, it was time for some relaxation at the pool–no tension from back home, just the glorious sunshine on my face. I sat back and felt joy seeing my kids' smiles. Their main agenda during our stay was to eat at Whataburger and In-N-Out to do a comparison challenge. This might have been the highlight of their trip.

Saturday we spent the day at the water park with Jasmine. My kids are like fish–they love the water as much as I do. After another incredible day of seeing their faces filled with excitement, Sunday quickly came, and we had to say our goodbyes to head back to Colorado.

On the way to Arizona, we had seen many billboard signs featuring "The Thing". We joked about it, so on the way back, we just had to find out what this "thing" was. We took a detour and decided to make a pit stop. The "thing" turned out to be a large souvenir shop with a zombie in a coffin that strangely attracts thousands of tourists passing through. We got a good laugh, and the mystery was solved. But realizing we were in a time crunch to make it back on schedule, we quickly had to hit the road.

As I started driving, the thought of returning home instantly tugged at me. My anxiety started to increase, as mixed emotions made me sick to my stomach. In just those few days, I realized something was missing in my life. It wasn't just the sunshine I was craving, it was the peace within myself. I had to figure out what makes me happy and what I really wanted, even if that meant walking away from a four-year relationship. The tough questions played through my mind: *Do I really want to show my daughters that this is how they should be treated? Is this how I want my son to grow up and treat his future partner? How many times do I have to keep picking up the pieces and starting over?* I had already moved five times prior to my current living situation. All of these thoughts ran through my head on the drive back home.

Ultimately, I made the decision to continue to do what is best for me and my kids. My advice to anyone is to listen to that inner voice and your gut and make the hard decisions. It won't be easy in the beginning, but you will look back and be thankful you did. Oh, and by the way, we made it back to Colorado Springs a little before 5:30 a.m. Monday morning, and I was able to open the doors to the daycare at 6. Talk about "just in the nick of time".

Wanda Ortiz

Hi, I'm Wanda. I'm from Puerto Rico by birth, but moved to the United States at four years old when my dad joined the Army. At 32, I followed in his footsteps and served in the Colorado Army National Guard for ten memorable years.

In my spare time, I enjoy anything fitness related. I love going on biking adventures, hiking the incline, and have completed multiple 5K, 10K, and Spartan races. I also recently started filling my time with modeling opportunities and participating in fashion shows. And I am passionate about volunteering for causes that are dear to my heart.

A Man of Joy

By Jasmine Rasch

Joshua Robert Norcutt

22.06.1979 – 25.02.2023

Traveled to his next destination with a "smile on his face" in the comfort of his bed in Eugene, OR, on February 25th, 2023. He is survived by his loving mother, Linda Norcutt, and many more loved ones. Art was his lifelong passion, along with glass blowing and, later on, beekeeping. But his biggest joys in life were, of course, his girls. He loved them more than life itself. Indie and Jasmine were who he lived for.

*M*y grandmother's only son, my great aunt's nephew, my mom's "baby daddy", mine and my sister's dad: Joshua Robert Norcutt.

My dad was no man to be afraid of. Though he was 6'2" and looked like he could take on anyone, he was really just a big teddy bear. He was the type of person to walk into a room and everyone's faces would light up, ready to hear what jokes he had in store. He also wasn't the type of guy you had to fake laugh around because quite frankly, his jokes were *always* funny. No matter how crazy they were, everyone was always in stitches. My dad was a big people pleaser, so he was all about making someone's day no matter what situation they were in.

My dad didn't live in a luxury house. It may sound crazy, but he actually preferred his cute, small space behind a nice tattoo shop. It may have been tiny, but he made it work. You had to cut through the tiny bedroom to get to the even smaller bathroom, and the kitchen was barely big enough to squeeze two people. Everyone was shocked that he lived in such a small place considering his size, but he made it feel roomy and was content with where he was at. There was actually a time where he shared this space with two others, Jasmine and Jay. But most of the time, it was just Dad and his Gracie girl, and luckily for her, there was a yard to run around and play with other dogs.

Now, not to sound a bit dramatic, but my dad had his fair share of girlfriends, situationships, and more. You could say he was quite popular while I was growing up. I don't remember many of his girlfriends–a few I liked, a few not so much– but Jasmine might have been one of my favorites. I know it's quite strange for me to have a favorite ex-girlfriend, especially with the same name as me. And I never thought the day would come for me to like one so much.

My dad and Jasmine had been together for about a year before I flew down to visit them for a couple weeks. The trip was fun, but I felt like I didn't get to experience much with my dad, or get to know Jasmine or her son Jay, so I came back again for a month. This time it was much more meaningful–I discovered how much Jasmine and I had in common outside of our name and got to know Jay very well. I'm glad I spent that time there. One night all four of us were playing dominoes, and I asked them, "Do you guys ever play games when I'm not here?" Jay responded, "Jasmine, when you're not here we're like three strangers living in the same house who barely talk to each other, but when you're here, it feels like we're a complete family." That has always stuck with me. All of my life, I've lived alone with my mom, so I've never experienced a family dynamic where we all do fun stuff together. At that moment, I felt like I was finally getting the chance, and I didn't want it to end.

My dad wanted me to live with him more than anything. I would hear stories about him cleaning his house, talking about how excited he was that I was going to come stay there. This was a bit after he and Jasmine, unfortunately, broke up. They weren't enemies, but as my dad put it, they "drifted apart", and he needed some time to himself. I think this was good for him as it gave him time to reflect on a lot and focus on his interests. He even went to a Pink Floyd concert that he wouldn't stop talking about.

My dad struggled with addiction for a very long time. I was too young to understand what that truly meant, but recognized that what he was doing was wrong. He tried to convince my sister and I that we had a normal childhood. I'm not going to get into details, but "normal" was not what you would call the things we saw. Despite his addiction, he still did what he could to show my sister and I how much he loved us. Though he didn't have much to spare, he was constantly spending money on things for us. One of my favorite memories was how much he loved a popsicle in the summer. He may have been a bit too tired to get up, but when the ice cream truck came around, there he was with five bucks, ready to get us both a sweet treat.

As my sister and I got older, my dad started to work on himself. My mom never believed that he would fight his addictions for my sister and I, but he proved her wrong. He cherished his girls so much that he would drop anything in a heartbeat, if it meant he got a chance to do something for us, or even just to see us.

As far as I can remember, it's always been my dad, my sister Indie, and my Grandma Boop (or Grandma Linda). We did everything together–from camping, small vacation trips, going to the beach–we did it all. Indie and I have different moms, so the chance to hang out with my sister has always been special to me. We never fought, just bickered, until my grandma put us in check. She used to play the silent game with us a lot, and whoever won earned five bucks. We may have driven her crazy, and still do a bit, but she loves us and definitely spoils us when she can.

My Grandma Boop isn't your typical cookie-making, sweater-giving, grandma. She's actually really great and fun to be around. She is a hard worker and deserves everything she's worked for. She's got the nicest car I've ever seen and is always up to do something fun. Mind you, her idea of fun isn't going for a walk or playing a board game like you'd expect. She recently flew me to Florida just to ride roller coasters with her at Busch Gardens. My grandma and my sister have their fair share of adventures too. One time she took Indie and my dad on an exciting trip to Las Vegas. She truly does deserve the world, and she doesn't get enough credit for all the things she has gone through.

Though my dad never wanted to do anything major with his life, he had a passion for art until his final days. He was never in it for the money, but simply for doing something he loved. If there's anything my dad taught me, it was that no amount of money is worth working in a miserable environment. Part of his love for art was glassblowing. He made pipes and whatnot, but my favorite of the things he created were his pendants. When I was pretty young, my dad wanted to do something special with Indie and I, so he stood behind me and guided me through making a beautiful heart pendant. I will cherish it forever.

My dad was always staying busy and loved doing activities with others. Beekeeping was his most recent hobby. He saw bees as amazing creatures and would remind me how without bees, there would be no us. When he first got into it, he sent Indie and I many movies of bees and photos of honeycombs. My sister asked him, "Whose bees are those?" He then responded with, "Woah, woah, woah, woah! Nobody owns the bees! They just have caretakers."

My dad had a lot of things, but nothing out of the ordinary. (Well, there was a dead bird in his fridge when we went through his house, but that is a story for another day). His crystals and rocks were his favorite little trinkets. My dad was a great rock hunter and found some of the most beautiful ones out there. He cherished these pieces, and they were sent down to my sister and I when he passed away.

The end of my dad's life was filled with love and joy, from friends in other countries, to people he no longer spoke to, and even the girls at the smoothie shop down the street from his house. People all over enjoyed his company–joy was all around him. The day I found out about his passing I couldn't help but think about those who might not know. Finding out this heartbreaking news was devastating, but breaking it to other people was even harder.

On the day of my dad's cremation, people came from hours away to say goodbye and celebrate his life. When it was time to let go, my sister and I kissed him on the forehead, and sent him off with all the love we had to give. Everyone around did. Seeing how many people were there for him showed just how loved this man was despite his battles. He helped and touched so many lives of others who were struggling. "Angel" by Jimi Hendrix played as they sent him in. The room was full.

My dad was the most kindhearted soul out there and is still touching lives even after his passing. He watches over my sister and I, and will continue to, until our time comes to join him. I look forward to seeing him in the afterlife. He has been, and always will be there for his loved ones—no matter what. He had so much love to share with everyone and will forever continue spreading it.

Jasmine Rasch

Hi, I'm Jasmine. I am currently finishing up highschool online, while working in a cute boutique called, The Annex.

In my free time, I like to read and crochet. I'm currently working on a blanket that is taking me quite a while–and while I do so, I enjoy watching *The Office* or anything on the Adult Swim Network.

Later in life, I would love to study psychology and sociology. But my "Plan B" is to be a nail tech. I have already been doing nails on myself and friends for the past four months and plan to continue growing in this art.

Breaking the Damn Dam

By Magnus Downs

A little encouragement goes a long way. Someone to push you in a direction when you're lost can be a bright light in even the darkest of places. A stagnant river with a dam stopping the flow just needs a surge of water, and that can come from anywhere. Once that water gets moving, it goes where it wants to as fast as it can.

From an early age, I've known what it's like to be alone—truly alone. I was homeschooled from preschool all the way up to fourth grade. This, paired with the fact that I moved houses every year, made it impossible for me to make friends. Well, I say that those were the reasons, but, truth be told, I was never allowed to leave the house. I was fully sheltered. But, I have five siblings, so that shouldn't be that bad, right? Wrong. I felt like they mostly all hated me. Not as you would think normal siblings "hate" each other but a genuine hate. My older brother never talked to me unless he was making fun of my weight. My older sister liked to hit me and shove my head into cabinets. My younger siblings were not quite old enough to talk to, and when they were, they just joined in with the older siblings. So for me it was always hatred or the quiet. For some reason, I always hated the quiet more.

When I was in fourth grade, my parents started going through rough patches like I had never seen before. I always thought of them on a teeter-totter for divorce. My mom wanted to start working herself, so there was no more time for homeschooling. This meant that when I finished 4th grade, I had to go to public school for the first time. Take a fish out of a fish tank and throw him in the ocean, and he'll do great, I bet.

I was 11 years old. Double digits. At the time, that was so amazing to me. I couldn't believe it—as if I was gonna get facial hair and grow six feet tall. I was in fifth grade. I was looking forward to sixth grade because I could start playing football. My dad loved football. Most men did where I'm from—the great state of Texas. Just as they say, "everything is bigger in Texas", every son's need to impress their father is bigger there. As far back as I can remember, I was getting thrown a football from my dad in our backyard, only feeling good when I could run fast enough and catch it perfectly. I could always look back if the ball was in my hands and see my dad happy. "Nice catch! You're gonna be a star tight end." But if the ball was on the ground, I would see my dad looking anywhere but at me. "Again! Hurry up and throw it back!" I wonder what he really thought in those moments. *How did he truly feel about me?*

My dad had his own issues that he took out on me. He was a severe alcoholic, and had been for years. I'm not too sure when it started, but I was way too young to remember. He would get black-out drunk just about every night. That's when he would teach me what he called "lessons" on football. He would say that he wanted me to be tough. Getting down into a three-point stance, he would tackle me full force and beat on me. He would say that if I could handle him, I could handle any player on the field. That's ironic to look back on, because he gave me more bruises than any player ever did.

I was a very chubby kid. I ate way too much. Sure, I was prepping for football, but no amount of working out could combat the amount of food I consumed. I just ate and ate and ate, and I couldn't stop. Kids bullied me, called me the fat kid, to say the least, but for the most part the bullying in 5th grade was pretty tame. Nothing I couldn't handle. As long as I was good at football the next year, who would care? So I kept eating and practicing football.

By that time, I was as big as a house. My dad hadn't gotten any better, and my mom couldn't handle him anymore. She had kicked him out many times before, but this time was different. I could tell, even then, that I wouldn't see him for a long time. This was hard for me. Even though he wasn't the best father, he was *my* father. Who would I try to impress? I stopped practicing football that summer. I didn't stop eating though. I was so lost and depressed, just stuffing my face to pass the time.

Summer ended, but football, and bullies started. I still wanted to try and play football, because how could I give that up when it was all I'd ever wanted for so long. I made the team as a right guard lineman. I played well because of my size, but no one on the team cared about that. They all cared about how fat I was. Unfortunately, they weren't the only ones. Everyday after football practice, I would walk from the field to the showers, absolutely drained. There was always this group of kids that would be somewhere between the field and the school, pointing and laughing at me. I thought this was the worst thing, until they started throwing rocks at me. Every day. After a big rock hit me on the side of my head and I bled alot, I started to leave my pads and helmet on. Though they stopped the rocks from hurting me physically, I still felt hurt by it all. I didn't want to be called fat by all these kids. I didn't want to be called fat by my team. I didn't want to play the fat position in football.

I didn't want to be fat.

Football season came to an end, and nothing had changed for me, except that I hated myself. I didn't know who I was. I didn't have my dad to try and emulate to make him proud. I didn't have any clue what I wanted to do or what would make me happy. Honestly, I hadn't really thought about it. At this point, all I *did* know was that I wanted to lose weight. I wanted to be skinny. That would make me happy. I could play a different position in football. No one would bully me. I'd have friends. Maybe girls would like me. Maybe *I* would like me. So that's what I focused on. It's what I became obsessed with. I barely ate. I worked out for hours a day. Losing weight became *everything* I thought about.

Seventh grade. I was much skinnier, but I was not happy. The bullies stopped bullying me about my weight. We actually became friends, if you want to call it that. I gave up my dad as a person to try and impress and replaced him with them. Football started and I told the coach I wanted a different position. The first game came and I was still on the line. The coaches wanted me to gain the weight back and enticed me daily to do so. They got mad when I ran extra laps and when they would see me in the cafeteria not eating anything. I thought they would give in eventually and take me off the line, but I was not going to win this game of chicken. Football season came to an end again. I wanted to play basketball next. I thought I was skinny and fast enough to make the team, but I tried out and didn't make it. The coaches told me it was because they wanted me to focus on football. At this point, I was really starting to hate football but wouldn't admit it to myself. I was trying to hold onto that part of my dad. So I thought what any rational person would think–I needed to get skinnier. I started hanging out more with my old bullies. They weren't the best company. They partied. They drank. They smoked. And I picked up their habits. But that wasn't all I picked up. I started purging and cutting myself. The year went by and so did the summer. I had gotten worse and worse, blinded in a shroud of my hatred, depression, and obsession.

Eighth grade. I started football, but instead of taking me off the line, the coaches just didn't play me. I guess they figured if I didn't like it, I would gain weight or something. The season ended and nothing changed. This year I wanted to get a girlfriend. I thought that would make me happy. That's just what I was missing—a girl. A girl would definitely make me happy and trying to get one would be easy. Chasing girls wouldn't cause me any problems, right? I found myself crushing on this girl in my art class. She was nice to me, for the most part, but never talked to me unless it was about a class project. She was lazy, like most kids, and didn't like doing her assignments, even for art. So, I'm not proud of it, but I did her art projects for her, thinking it would make her like me.

Valentine's day came around, and I had my plan. I had gotten her favorite candy and wrote her a card. I showed up to class, left it on her desk next to mine, and sat, waiting for her to get there and read it. When she finally got to class and saw it, she looked over at her friend on the other side and said, "I bet it's from Gavin." I heard that and wished I had shrunk to the size I felt in that moment so that she couldn't see me. Gavin was the wide receiver on the team, and I had already been extremely envious of the way he looked before I found out she had a crush on him. She opened the card and read it, turned and looked at me for just a split second, then looked back at the card. She handed me the candy and the card without even saying a word. She never spoke to me again after that. I ate the candy when I got home from school that day. I was more sad about eating the candy than the rejection.

Highschool. The parties got worse. I got worse. I only stayed in football that season for two weeks before quitting. I couldn't handle not eating and all the exercise. Truth be told, I'd grown to hate football. I hated my father even more.

Even though my older brother and I weren't close, he started driving me to school instead of me riding the bus. He played music in the car that I had never heard before. I had always listened to what my friends were listening to and never gave it any thought. Nothing had really ever struck a chord with me. Something about what he played resonated. Grunge. Nirvana specifically caught my attention. I started listening to music on my own, trying things out. I fell in love with rock. On our car rides, I would show my brother what I had been listening to, and we talked about music a lot after that. One day, he took me to his room after school and showed me his CD collection. That's when I saw it—his bass sitting in the corner. I asked if I could play it, and he said yes. I picked it up and had no idea what I was doing, but I loved just holding it. My brother told me I should get an instrument after that. I knew exactly what I wanted. I stayed up all night looking at guitars. I found an Epiphone SG that I just knew was me. This was the first time things started to feel like me. I knew I had to have it. I got a job working for my grandpa in construction, painting new houses for months after school until I saved up enough. I bought the guitar and sat in my room as often as I could, teaching myself to play. I had a new obsession—a passion. Music made me happy for the first time in a long time. I didn't stop at guitar—I learned bass, drums, piano, ukulele, anything I could get my hands on, really. Though the realization may seem small, this was the first big step in the right direction.

So everything was fixed, right? Wrong. Though I had discovered a true side to me, I still had a lot of trauma and bad behaviors to overcome. At this point in my life, I was a sophomore in highschool. My mom pulled me and my younger siblings out of the great state of Texas and into the rocky mountain high of Colorado. My brother was in college and wanted to finish his degree before moving, and my sister decided to move in with her boyfriend, so they stayed behind. I was now the oldest sibling in the house. Everything was new. Brand new school and, I figured, brand new me. Only one issue: COVID-19. Where I had lived in Texas, the town was so small that no one was really affected by COVID, so school went on like normal. In Colorado, this was not the case. Online school meant no way of making friends. Not only no friends, but no one at all. It was just me and my siblings and mom. Day after day, only solitude. I had grown to hate quiet. It brought back memories of being homeschooled in elementary school. Though the bullying and abuse from my older siblings had gone away at this point, it was replaced by my mom.

I felt like my mom neglected me as a child, but now she was definitely paying attention to me. She progressively got more strict and more aggressive towards me. Now that we were out of Texas and my father was gone, she told me she could finally start living her life. So when she wasn't at work, she wasn't home. That meant that

I had to step up my responsibilities, as she put it. I essentially parented my younger siblings–I picked them up from school, I cooked all the meals, and I cleaned the house. Truth be told, I was your standard 1950's housewife. And what happened to wives back then when they weren't perfect all the time? Well, anytime my mom was home consisted of screaming, slapping me in the face, and belittling comments. After her tantrums were said and done, it was back to work. I couldn't handle it, and soon came my first suicide attempt.

To blame my mother for any of my suicide attempts is wrong. The pressure was just too much. And no matter what anyone does to me, it will always be my choice whether or not to give up. At this time in my life, I made that choice. I went to my mom's bathroom and took every pill in her medicine cabinet. My mom found all the pills missing when she got home from work, not 15 minutes later. I woke up in the hospital getting my stomach pumped. I was off to the mental hospital for a week-long stay.

During my hospitalization, I met several other kids, but one specific girl stood out to me. She had self-harm scars all over her body. All the other kids said she looked scary, but I tried to picture her without the scars. I started to talk to her, and she was the sweetest girl I had ever met. She told me about why she was in there with me, and it broke me down to hear it. At the end of her story, she told me about how she felt now, and I'll never forget it. She said the strongest people have faced the most difficult situations and reminded me that we were both strong.

I went back home after a week and decided that no matter how hard things got, I could be strong. I worked and worked all through the remainder of the school year and summer. COVID had died down, masks were worn less and less, until the mandate was gone, and I was finally back in school again, where I could make friends. Not to say it was easy. It took me a while to find one. But when I did, I fell back into my old ways. I started partying again, religiously. I started numbing the burdens and pain the wrong way. But, as long as I kept up with school and all my chores, no one paid attention. Day after day, I spiraled worse and worse. I was sick all of the time from partying and not eating. This went on for the rest of the school year with no hesitation.

The following summer, my mom had gotten a new job a few hours away, so another move, another new school–*alone again*. But moving did force me to stop all of my bad behaviors due to lack of resources.

Junior year. I was so excited to take a graphic design class, but all the spots were filled up. My counselor gave me the option of photography or cinematography instead. The idea of filming movies sounded fun and easy, so I chose cinematography. When I walked into class on my first day, the teacher pulled me aside and told me the class might be difficult, having not taken the prerequisite intro class that I didn't know I needed. He wanted to make sure that I wasn't lost on how to complete my assignments, so he paired me with another student who had been filming shorts for years. The student was already working on a film and took me down to observe him recording a scene. Watching the film process sparked my interest. I stayed up all night researching cinematography.

The next day at the library, I checked out several books on cinematography, acting, script writing, cameras–anything that caught my eye on the subject. I finished them all in about a week, really anxious to be more involved. The next time my partner went to film a scene, I asked if I could do some takes with the camera. Because he was close to finishing filming, he let me. There was a fight scene in the script and he stepped back, allowing me to demonstrate what I could do. He ended up loving my camera work so much, that he used it in the film. My teacher was also impressed–he asked me to work on more projects by myself. I started watching movies through a different lens. I started to write scripts for fun. I started to really enjoy the art of cinematography.

But I also floundered back to my old ways, though not as bad as before. One night, I went to a smaller party. This party didn't last too long, but I drank a lot and was then invited to go to the movies with a few other people. Not wanting to go home yet, I went along. While at the movies I drank more and passed out. I woke up to two girls I didn't know very well, pulling me out of my seat to leave because the movie was over. They helped me to their car and said they were going to take me home. I was handed another drink, but this one hit me differently—it definitely wasn't just alcohol. We stopped at a house, where they told me they needed to run in before taking me home. I was beginning to have trouble standing. As they helped me inside, I noticed that one stopped to turn on the house alarm. I was then told I had to spend the night, because if I tried to leave it would wake up their parents. By this point I couldn't walk at all. I felt completely out of it. I was taken to a room where they proceeded to sexually assault me. In the morning, I was sent out the front door to walk home. This is when I decided to never party again.

Senior year. I started to get more and more serious with myself. I'd like to say I purposely changed, but I think it was my hobbies and better company that did it inadvertently. My only friends were my cinematography teacher and my older brother, who finished college and moved to Colorado. I started focusing on my passions and staying strong for myself. I combined my love for music and my love for cinematography by filming shorts and writing/recording the soundtracks for all of them. For the first time, I was proud of myself. Near the end of my senior year, I finished a short film that I consider my best project. My teacher told me about a film festival in New York that he wanted me to submit it to. I sent it in and figured nothing would happen. For a while, nothing did.

In the midst of all of this, my mom only got worse. Nothing was ever good enough for her anymore. It didn't matter if I did everything right, it still felt like I was the anti-Christ. She expected me to do all of the things around the house, but also required me to have a job. I was actually happy about that part. I would have money and could save up for a car. Not having a car meant biking to work. I wouldn't have minded, but doing so on top of everything else was stretching me pretty thin. On my way to work one day, a car came out and swerved to miss a dog in the street, hitting me instead. I laid on the side of the road, bleeding, while the car sped away. No one even pulled over to help me. After lying there in pain, I pickled myself up and walked home. My mom insisted I quit my job, because it was too dangerous. But when I healed up a few weeks later, she wanted me to get a job again. This time, I had to quit after a week, because she didn't like the schedule. She kept doing this over and over again. I really wanted a job, but I couldn't handle all the stress.

Graduation. I was ready to start college, but wasn't sure what to major in, which was stressing me out. Being out of school was supposed to give me more time, but my mom became even more overbearing. She said that with more time, I could do more things for the family. I felt so alone, with no friends and nowhere to go.

Then one day, the most amazing thing happened to me. Reese Walton walked into my life. She was different from anyone else I'd ever met. She didn't make me feel small, belittle, or question me. In fact, she didn't show even an ounce that she didn't care for me. Reese was so funny that she made me laugh harder than ever, so smart that she was always right, so beautiful that she captivated my eyes, even in my dreams, and so loving that she became my home. She became my everything.

I'm happy to say all of this is still true and always will be. Reese's family was also amazing. For the first time, I saw a family who loved each other. They accepted me as if they'd known me their whole life and cared for me as one of their own. I could argue with Reese back and forth all day about whether or not I deserved it, but at the end of the day, I'm lucky to have them all.

Near the end of summer, I received an email from the film festival—I got in and was going to New York! I was being recognized for something that *I* did. I returned home with awards in several categories: horror, short films, and music. But I also gained a new perspective about myself. I decided to go to college for cinematography and music. I knew that nothing was guaranteed, but I needed to pursue what I love.

I'd like to say music, film, and love fixed all my other problems. They didn't. But what they did do was show me who I am: my authentic self. The me *I* want to be. They gave me the internal strength to work on my other problems and see them for what they are. They gave me direction. They gave me confidence.

I'd like to thank my brother for giving me the gift of music. I'd like to thank my cinematography teacher for introducing me to film. And I'd like to thank Reese and her family for showing me love. Even though they didn't know what they were doing at the time, they all started me on this path to a more positive me. I finally like what I'm doing and where I'm going. I like me. I love me.

I know there is a lot of sadness in my story, but hardship molds us into who we are. I would never trade the difficult experiences, because they led me to the joys and love I have now. No matter how hard life can be, there will always be worth in moving forward, even if you can't see it at the time. My life isn't over, and my story isn't anywhere near fully written. There will be more sadness and more hardships to come, but there will also be more joy and love. So, never give up on your life and cut the possibilities short. I'm going to keep living, and if you take anything away from my story, it is that you should too.

Magnus Downs

My name is Magnus. I am a cinematography student and aspiring musician. My typical day involves working on music, watching movies, and hanging out with my girlfriend, Reese.

I have a passion for both music and cinema. Leonardo DiCaprio is my favorite actor, and I absolutely love *The Evil Dead* series. My dream is to be a director and screenplay writer of thrillers and horror films, like my idol, Sam Raimi. I hope to one day open my own movie production studio in Hollywood, where I will write, direct and produce my movies and their sound scores.

'Miss' Me More

By Reese Walton

When I was younger, you could say I was a little boy crazy. I'm pretty sure I had a crush on a new boy every year from six years old to fifteen. Just like any typical little girl, I dreamed of having a prince charming someday like I saw in the Disney princess movies. I always knew what my ideal love life would be...but I never knew how much of an impact it'd actually have on my life.

I remember every single crush I had during my elementary school years. None of them liked me back. I was always the girl chasing them at recess, confessing my "love" when I got the courage, and writing them notes in class. My best friend told a boy in my fifth-grade class that I liked him, and he ran away screaming. But, at that age, I thought that the chase was a part of the journey of love, so I didn't really mind.

In middle school, my thought process and confidence changed drastically. I told my parents and friends that I didn't care what anyone else thought of me, as long as I liked myself. Well, that's easier said than done. Anyone (and everyone) who has experienced middle school knows that insecurities and over-thinking come as a packaged deal. I was twelve, so cliques, boys, and drama were all I cared about. I still had many crushes throughout these years, but being constantly rejected started to have an impact on my confidence. Boys would jokingly come up to me during lunch to "ask me out". When I'd say yes, they'd go back and start laughing with their friends. If my friends tried to talk to a boy for me and suggest we start hanging out, they'd scoff and reply, "Ew, why would I wanna do that, Reese is ugly." I was always a joke to them. So, if I ever had any crushes after that, I stayed quiet. However, my older brother, Samuel, had a girlfriend at the time. I saw how well he treated her and how happy they were together. I told everyone that someday, I wanted a guy who treated me as well as Samuel treated his girlfriend.

High school came, and I had less and less of an obsession with boys. I was still what everyone would call a hopeless romantic, but I had lost the previous confidence in myself. I didn't think I was pretty enough to get a boy. At fifteen, I technically wasn't allowed to date for another year anyway, but I still dreamed about it. My parents had also recently divorced; their relationship was filled with a lot of fighting and tears, so the thought of marriage didn't appeal to me like it used to. Social media had also become the primary communication for dating–Snapchat especially. Instead of someone asking for your number, boys would ask for your Snapchat handle instead. It was very rare that you'd find a teenager without Snapchat downloaded on their phone. And while Snapchat can be convenient to use on occasion, the app makes it hard to have genuine conversations. In my opinion, social media has a negative impact on social interaction in general, especially for teens, making it harder to communicate with peers in real life. It definitely impacted me and my social anxiety with boys at this time.

When I turned sixteen, my parents finally allowed me to date. Except it wasn't as exciting as I'd hoped it would be. I didn't have a crush on any boys, nor did any like me, so nothing had actually changed. Sure, I talked to some boys I was interested in here and there, but they always turned out to be the same. I quickly discovered that there is always going to be the boy who only wants you for one thing: your body. And that's a hard fact to accept. Almost every conversation I had with a boy ended up with him asking me to send inappropriate photos. This was so upsetting. I'd cry and wish that they wanted me for who I actually was as a person. Of course, I never sent the photos. I'd block whoever it was, be sad for a bit, and move on with my day. But my idea of what love was seemed more like a fairytale as time went on–something that's only real in romance books and movies.

By the time I was seventeen, my friends had all had relationship experience. I started to wonder if there was something wrong with me. *How come everyone else can find someone that they're compatible with, but I can't?* Deep down, it truly bothered me. I tried to convince myself that I didn't actually care that much. I eventually went on my first date, just a few months shy of turning eighteen. (Well, *if* you call playing video games a date.) We had been calling each other for hours on end before he actually asked me out and then eventually to be his girlfriend. It felt good that he had pursued me first, because that had never happened to me before. I was so anxious when he picked me up. I brought my dog with me to calm me down. I even experienced my first kiss. But, long story short, I found out he had been seeing other girls at the same time, so I broke things off with him. The hope I had in finding love continued to decrease.

At eighteen, I had almost given up on finding someone. Boys would ask to hang out every once in a while, but I felt too insecure to ever actually follow through with it. I told myself and my friends that I didn't care about being in a relationship anymore. I was fine with being single. I started focusing on myself, and I realized that I needed to like myself before worrying about someone else liking me. I learned how to be content with being alone and how to become confident with my looks again. I began to understand that what I was hoping for in love *wasn't* too much to ask, and I should always set standards for what I deserve.

Shortly after, I met Magnus. I remember him messaging me, calling me gorgeous, and asking for my number. I gave it to him, honestly not thinking much of it. We started texting back and forth here and there, but, at the time, I still wasn't actively pursuing a relationship, so I wasn't really expecting the conversations to go anywhere. But I noticed right away that Magnus truly seemed interested in talking to me and listening to my ideas and opinions.

He made a point to ask me how my day was, or even how I felt in general. I felt like he was interested in me, for *me*. Eventually, he suggested going on a date. I had started to develop feelings for him, but didn't want to admit that yet. I was afraid of getting my hopes up.

I agreed to go on a date with Magnus, despite my reservations. We talked over the phone for two weeks before the day finally came. I woke up very early that morning due to lack of sleep and was extremely anxious. I had to convince myself not to cancel about five thousand times. I kept dwelling on everything that could go wrong, and all the past things that had happened. But I just kept telling myself that I'd be fine either way. Driving to his house, I felt sick to my stomach, but when I realized that his house was a twenty minute drive away, I felt better knowing I had time to calm myself down.

When I finally arrived, I got out of my car and was greeted with a huge smile on Magnus' face. We awkwardly said hello, then I followed him around to the big field behind his house where he had set up a picnic. We found ourselves lost in conversation about our interests and dreams in life, including the fears that come along with them. He encouraged me right away to believe in myself more, because he could tell that I didn't. Eventually, it started to rain, so we packed up the food and went inside to watch his favorite movie, *Wall-E*. We ended up missing the whole movie because we were too busy talking and throwing popcorn into each other's mouths. He kept trying to pop my knuckles, because I told him how much I hated it when people do that, and this naturally led us to holding hands.

As the night progressed, we went outside in hopes of stargazing. Unfortunately, it was very cloudy that night. But despite this, we laid down on the grass, looking at the sky, talking about the patterns of the clouds. I started to notice just how comfortable I felt with him. We were lying on our sides when it started to rain again. The drops were getting in my eyes, making it hard to see, so he pulled the hood of my sweatshirt over both of our faces. As we continued to talk, our lips would touch, and finally, we kissed.

I think it's safe to say that the first date went well, as we've now been together for almost a year. Magnus has been my biggest supporter since the day I met him and helped me learn a lot about myself. My positive experience with love has since influenced other areas that I've struggled in throughout my life. My lack of confidence and fear of failing had stopped me from pursuing my dreams. I realized that if I had given in to my anxiety and canceled my first date with Magnus, I would've never experienced the magic of these past eleven months. I never would have felt how much love I could share with another person or had the confidence to try other new things that could potentially be scary. Our relationship is an example of pursuing something, even if you're nervous or afraid of failing. My goal now, in my life, is to look at everything else with the same mindset. You'll never know how something is going to work out until you try. I want to try.

Reese Walton

My name is Reese. I have a passion for psychology and a deep interest in understanding the inner workings of the human mind. I enjoy exploring different theories and analyzing how and why people think and behave the way they do. In my free time, I enjoy reading articles on psychology or watching documentaries that delve into the subject.

I have an eye for photography and capturing the beauty in everyday moments. In my free time, I also enjoy writing short stories and essays that explore different aspects of life and the world. I love all animals, especially horses, and of course, my dog, Abbey.

How a Couple of Misfits Found Love: How a Miss Found her Mister

By Tabby Halsrud

"It's been ages since I've been noticed by a man. I'm starting to think I'm meant to be single for the rest of my life."

After two divorces and numerous wrong-fit dating situations, I was starting to lose hope that I'd ever find the kind of love I had been longing for. Past relationships left me feeling hurt and disappointed time and again; I've been used, judged, manipulated, cast aside, and betrayed. A girl can only take so much heartbreak before she starts to question if true love exists. After my second divorce, I experienced a very difficult three years of dating before finally embracing my singleness and independence. I took a break from dating that ended up lasting two years (which was about 18 months longer than I had anticipated). During that time, I focused on other aspects of my life that needed attention and continued my self-healing and personal growth journey.

I had heard the name *Garrett Goggans* several times before I ever met him. Since we were both entrepreneurs, we knew a lot of the same people. Garrett and I finally met at a social event where we ended up on the same trivia team (Go Pineapples!). About two weeks later, I attended a networking meeting as a guest, and it turned out that Garrett was the speaker. What I remember most about that day is that I found a lot of value in the content he delivered, and his talk made me cry. Garrett shared how important it is to know what we want but that knowing it isn't enough–we also have to ensure our vibration and energy is aligned with that desire. While I believed the validity of this statement, I wasn't even sure what I wanted. So I asked him, "What advice would you give someone who doesn't *know* what they want?" His response was, "You really do know what you want. Your limiting thoughts and beliefs are blocking it." This hit me like a punch to the gut, and tears of truth fell in the car on the way home. I had been working on healing some old wounds and was having a hard time letting myself envision a better future. I didn't have faith that I could receive what I wanted, personally or professionally, because I didn't believe I deserved it. I knew I had some more work to do within myself.

The following month, the Universe brought Garrett and I together again when we were both invited by a mutual colleague to join a study group on positive intelligence. I was intrigued by the opportunity to support the shifts I was working to make within myself, as well as learning another tool that I could use with my clients. Our pod of four met weekly for two months studying the techniques, practicing them on ourselves, and discussing what we were learning. Over that two months together, Garrett and the others provided wonderful support for me as I continued to navigate my own healing. He saw me in some really challenging and vulnerable moments. I noticed an attraction to him and a curiosity about him that I quickly dismissed. I was still pretty deep in my self-healing process and didn't feel ready to explore any kind of relationship.

Over the following several months, my interaction with Garrett was limited to Facebook and the occasional engagement with each other's posts. We made a few attempts to meet up for coffee, but those plans always fell through. Almost a year after our participation in the positive intelligence study group, the Universe set into motion a series of events that would begin the evolution of our relationship from colleagues, to friends, to something more.

Garrett reached out to reschedule a coffee date we had canceled several weeks prior. In that text exchange, I mentioned that I was moving that weekend and he offered to help (ummm, how sweet was that!). The move was very emotional for me, because it was unplanned and unwanted; tears fell as soon as we started moving my stuff into my friend's house. After we had gotten a bulk of the heavy items inside, one of the ladies helping with the move asked Garrett if he would put my bed frame together for me. I looked at him and affirmed, "If you do that, I will love you forever..." I was feeling overwhelmed, and I felt grateful about having one less thing to do.

About two weeks later, Garrett and I finally had our rescheduled coffee meeting and easily fell into conversation that was deep, vulnerable, and real but also very comfortable. I noticed an attraction to him again, but because I was still feeling like an emotional mess, I quickly dismissed it. *Who would be interested in someone who doesn't have their shit together?* In the weeks following, the frequency of our interactions through Facebook increased. When Garrett made a post requesting speakers for his storytelling event, I expressed interest, and we agreed to meet for coffee to discuss it. In that conversation, we also shared our business struggles with each other. I disclosed how I had been ignoring my callings and the fears and blocks I had been working through. As he had always done before, he created a safe space for me to show up fully in all my confusion and struggle. He encouraged me to step into my calling and allow things to unfold. I was incredibly grateful for our conversation and for the insights that came in the following days. With Garrett, I always felt safe to show up as myself and speak my truth without fear of judgment. Garrett had a special way of delivering truth that I needed to hear, right when I needed to hear it. He had become one of my trusted truth tellers and a cherished friend.

By that point, I had decided that I was ready to explore a relationship, but since I am strongly opposed to online dating, I wasn't exactly sure how it would happen. I was feeling disappointed after a few uncomfortable interactions with men who made unwelcome, over-the-top advances toward me. As irritating as these situations were, they sure did help me update my plea to be seen by a man. Those men saw me in all the wrong ways, and I was longing to be seen on a whole different level. One morning, I was feeling especially frustrated about how long I had been single and was exploring the topic in my journal, asking directly: *"Why am I still single?"* Almost immediately, the response came: *"It's not all about you. He's not ready yet. Be patient."* At the time, I didn't know who "he" was. But that was an important piece of guidance to receive. It helped me shift my perspective and lean into patience, trusting that I'd meet the man I was supposed to when the time was right.

The day of Garrett's storytelling event, I noticed an unexpected eagerness to see him again. That night, I gave my talk and chatted with him for a few minutes. Before I left the event, I asked if we could get a selfie together. When I got home, I scrolled through the photos I had taken that night, and when I came to our selfie, I paused. I was struck by how intimate our positioning was and how much we were leaning into each other. I also noticed the big smile I had on my face and the intense attraction I felt to him. The thing that struck me the most was that we *looked* good together, and we looked like a couple! I imagined what it would be like to be together.

Then came my, "Oh shit" moment. *What do I do?* I wasn't sure how to navigate my attraction toward him. For one thing, I remembered him making prior statements that he wasn't interested in dating and didn't want a relationship. Another point of confusion for me was that I noticed I felt *calm* and *safe* when I was with him—and this was not what I was used to feeling when attracted to a man. I misunderstood this new and unknown energy—it made me second guess the nature of my attraction. What I didn't fully understand at the time was that I had done so much healing and growth in the relationship space, that physical attraction was no longer enough for me. The attraction I felt for Garrett went beyond the physical, which is why the energy felt different. I had been longing for the safety and acceptance that he had been providing me.

One thing that *was* clear to me was that in my desire to be seen by a man, I had completely missed the fact that Garrett had been seeing me at a whole other level all along. He had seen me at some of my darkest, most challenging moments but never judged me and always held safe space for me. He saw past the physical, beyond the messiness, and into my soul. I felt accepted, understood, and supported by him.

Two weeks after speaking at his storytelling event, Garrett and I again met for coffee. We had both been struggling with some "off" energy, and we knew that getting together would shift it. As soon as he walked into the coffee shop, I jumped up to hug him, and we immediately fell into deep conversation again. As always, we covered many topics, and eventually our conversation shifted to dating. We exchanged some of our past dating challenges and lessons. He mentioned that it was the second time the topic of dating had come up for him in a week's time. I suggested that anything that comes up twice in a short period of time may be guidance to explore. He asked, "What if you already know what the guidance is telling you?" I replied, "Well, then you get to decide what you want to do about it." I was feeling incredibly drawn to him at this point but was still uncertain what to do about my attraction. Hearing that he had recently talked about dating, with someone else, I naturally assumed he was interested in *someone else*.

Before we knew it, two and a half hours had gone by. I wanted to stay longer, but the establishment was closing. When we parted ways, our hug felt different–it seemed to linger a bit longer than usual. *Was that just me?* I wasn't sure. When we got home, our conversation continued through text, and we both acknowledged how much we enjoyed the night and how it felt like not enough time. We were both grateful for the conversation and the ability to just be present with each other. It didn't take many messages back and forth for me to begin to realize–*I think maybe he's interested in me too!* Then came the text that changed everything. He wrote, "Tabby, I think I need to give you a full confession. I'm very attracted to you. I suppose I should get that truth out in the open." I breathed a sigh of relief, smiled to myself, and replied that the attraction was mutual.

Within three weeks of our mutual confession, our connection had grown even stronger. We both knew without a doubt that we were brought together for a reason. Our souls found comfort, safety, and support in each other. We had a very strong foundation on which to build a relationship, and there was a "naturalness" and ease that existed between us. We mutually agreed to enter into a committed relationship, and when we went "Facebook official" with our status, we received an outpouring of support from our network. Many people who knew both of us affirmed our relationship; no one seemed all that surprised to hear about it. Some shared that they always thought we would make a good couple, a few said they had picked up on energy between us at one point or another, and others said it made so much sense for us to be together. We've often joked with each other, "Why didn't they clue us in?" But in reality, we know that our timing wasn't right until it *was* right. If we would have tried to initiate a relationship any earlier, it likely wouldn't have worked, and we would have ended up being just another casualty for each other. We both had additional healing and growth that we needed to do individually before we were ready to come together. The Universe accelerated our connections at just the right time, when we were both able to see each other in a whole new way and ready to explore what had been waiting so patiently to unfold.

This is the story of how Garrett and I came to be life partners. But it wouldn't have happened without all the work we did on ourselves beforehand. I had many unhealthy relationship patterns that I needed to unlearn and a lot of guilt, shame, and anger from past relationships that needed to be resolved first. I had to stop blaming others for past relationship failures and take accountability for my own mistakes and choices. I learned to forgive others for their transgressions and to forgive myself for mine. I had to *choose* not to remain beholden to old wounds and *let myself heal* from decades of hurt and betrayals, so I could learn to trust again. As much as I had wanted someone to choose me and to fight for me, I had to learn how to choose myself and fight for myself, first.

After we started dating, I was going back through some old journals and found this entry, written almost exactly two months before Garrett and I disclosed our attraction for each other:

Clarity on what I *do* want:

- *A loving, committed relationship with an available and safe man*
- *Willingness, effort, and desire for connection and intimacy*
- *Deep love beyond just attraction and desire*
- *Someone to provide emotional support and to help carry the load*
- *Kindness, compassion, and care*
- *Fun and laughter*
- *Quality time and conversation*
- *Affection, warmth, mutual nurturing*
- *Presence and attentiveness*
- *Passion*

- *Growth-mindedness and a desire to support each other's growth*
- *Balanced giving and receiving*
- *Emotional safety and allowance for each other's emotions*

These qualities are the foundation of the relationship that Garrett and I have been building. It's a relationship unlike anything I've ever experienced before, because we are integrating attraction and passion with honest communication, safety, trust, and love.

Toward the end of my two years of singlehood, I had a deep longing to experience love, and at times the sadness and loneliness felt unbearable. It was hard to be patient. I was approaching 50 and starting to believe it wasn't going to happen for me...that I was meant to be alone. But now, I don't even care how long it took for us to come together, because finding genuine love has been worth the wait. The thing is, we meet people exactly when we are supposed to meet them–no sooner and no later. If we aren't ready to *give and receive* real love, it's not going to flow into our life, regardless of how much we wish for it. My voyage to a life with Garrett ran parallel with the deep inner journey I took toward a transformed, more loving *me.*

Tabby Halsrud

Tabby Halsrud's soul is on a quest to provide guidance for people who want to grow beyond past relationship experiences and cultivate healthy, loving relationships now. The depth of Tabby's work persuades people to view their relationships as an important spiritual practice and an opportunity for growth. She inspires people to stretch beyond old patterns and arrive at fresh perspectives so they can show up more courageously with their loved ones. Tabby's clients validate feelings and genuinely express needs in their relationships. Tabby is a life-long student and passionately shares pieces of her story to inspire others through writing, blogging, speaking, and 1-1 guidance. Tabby has several years' experience coaching, facilitating and teaching many topics including personal growth and relationships. She has a Master's

Degree in Leadership and Training & Development. Tabby resides in Colorado with her beloved partner and their blended family and enjoys reading, journal writing, hiking, listening to live music, and dancing.

Tabby Halsrud
Relationship Cultivator and Author

https://linktr.ee/tabby_halsrud / thepaceofguidance@gmail.com

How a Couple of Misfits Found Love: How a Mister Found His Miss

By Garrett Goggans

J didn't want to date, at least that is what I told myself and anyone else who ventured down the relationship conversation. Why would I? After two failed marriages, I had immersed myself into a journey of personal healing and discovery. I was focused on building me, my brand, and my mission of helping others find success in whatever endeavor they were in. Not only was there little time to give to that sort of relationship, but it had also been my experience that dating would interrupt the sense of peace that I had finally found. At times, women would enter my life, challenging the very mantra I had adopted, but there was one specific person who would leave a profound impact on me.

I met Tabby at a trivia night organized by a mutual acquaintance, where we found ourselves on the same team. This arrangement allowed me the opportunity to gaze into her captivating crystal-blue eyes without it being awkward or me feeling too self-conscious. Her laughter had a way of lighting up the room, filling my heart with instant joy. Tabby exuded an energy unlike anything I had encountered before. Despite feeling a strong physical attraction towards her, I quickly dismissed it, reiterating to myself that I had no intention of pursuing a romantic relationship.

A few weeks later, Tabby and I would see each other again at a networking event I was giving a talk at. We had a brief conversation where I again noticed her energy and how different it was from anyone I had encountered. Though our interaction was short, her presence lingered in my thoughts throughout the day, once again questioning my dating beliefs. I quickly pushed the idea aside, going through the process of convincing myself that there wasn't the time, or a deep enough desire, to even think about having a relationship.

Some time elapsed before our paths crossed once more, affording us the opportunity to spend additional time together. We found ourselves among a group enrolled in a positive intelligence course, meeting weekly to delve into topics like our core beliefs and life blockers. As we shared insights and exchanged perspectives, I couldn't deny the allure of our discussions, craving more opportunities to connect on a deeper level. In fact, I may have even suggested the idea of arranging one-on-one meetings, though I ultimately failed to follow through due to my lingering apprehensions about pursuing a relationship.

Following the positive intelligence course, I underwent a profound period of healing and personal growth. Despite my insistence to myself, and others, that I wasn't ready to dive back into the dating scene, I could not ignore the internal tug pulling me in that direction. However, my attempts at dating fell short each time, leaving me unable to fully invest myself. One particular experience, where I allowed myself to become more involved, ended with me having to assert non-negotiable boundaries. While these encounters didn't involve Tabby, they reinforced my belief that relationships of this nature would disrupt the hard-earned peace I had cultivated and was determined to safeguard at all costs.

Eventually, Tabby and I crossed paths once again. We had been trying to coordinate a meet-up when she mentioned her upcoming move. While I'd like to attribute my helpful nature for the eagerness to lend a hand, truthfully, it was the prospect of seeing her again that sparked my excitement. What's more, learning that she would be just a short four-minute drive away only added to my anticipation. However, this time around, things felt different. Tabby's energy seemed to have shifted, and I couldn't shake the feeling that mine had too. It seemed we were both in a transitional phase, yearning for the right connections to help propel us forward again. Given our close proximity and shared mindset, it only made sense to commit to meeting more frequently, engaging in meaningful conversations as kindred spirits on a similar journey.

Something you learn quickly in a self-discovery journey is the number of people you hang out with will dwindle as you continue to grow. Initially, I believed our connection was merely an opportunity for like-minded individuals to engage in meaningful conversations. However, upon reflection, I must confess that there were deeper motivations at play. On our first meeting, I realized that we were able to easily jump into deep discussions feeling safe, heard, genuinely understood, and supported. This single interaction elevated my energy to new heights as well, a sensation I had seldom experienced. It was at that moment that my initial attraction to her intensified enough for me to take note.

My past marriages and relationships left me feeling like I was carrying the weight alone. The lack of mutual exchange was glaring, and the toxicity of these dynamics were undeniable. Yet, with Tabby, it was different. Despite her self-proclaimed "hot mess" status, she exuded a serene energy unlike any other. Feeling and experiencing a reciprocal exchange of energy, was a refreshing change. In previous encounters, I often found myself doing the heavy lifting, but with Tabby, it was a mutual exchange that left me craving more, eager to explore where this could lead.

Each time we got together our talks would prove to be deep and purposeful. My emotional attraction to Tabby grew more intense, and so did the physical. This was made obvious at a local speaking event that I host once a month. Tabby was going to give a talk, and the promotional image she used left me utterly captivated—I found myself unable to look away. The night of the event she looked amazing, I kept searching for her in the room so I could catch a glimpse. When she was presenting her talk, I must confess that my attention was somewhat diverted, as I found myself entranced by her "presence" in more ways than one.

Even though my levels of attraction were continuously increasing, there was still a battle being fought within, as to whether I wanted a relationship and, more importantly, if I was actually ready for one. The subject of dating had been brought up in a conversation I had with someone else that led me to believe it might be something that I was ready for–I was just too scared to admit it. Shortly after that conversation, I met with Tabby and the topic presented itself again.

The conversation topics between Tabby and I always flowed naturally. They almost felt inspired as opposed to intentional, so the fact that dating came up was more like a sign. By this time, the feelings I had for Tabby were pretty undeniable, and this particular talk was leading me down a path where I was going to have to make a choice. Where we were meeting was about to close, but Tabby would leave me with a final thought. If the pull to date is continuous, and the topic keeps coming up, it is a safe bet that it is time to take the leap.

I was pretty certain Tabby had no clue of my feelings that had been developing for her, so she probably didn't know that she had just given me advice on asking her out. Unfortunately, that conversation would have to happen next time, because the evening had come to an end. I didn't want to wait until next time though. The discussion continued through text, and my intuition was screaming at me to tell her how I felt, so I sent the message. I am not sure of the exact wording, but it was along the lines of I felt the need to be honest and transparent and expressed my attraction for her.

Much to my delight, and a little bit to my surprise, she expressed the same. However, now there were many different conversations that needed to be had.

Just because we announced our mutual attraction did not necessarily mean we were ready to just jump in the dating scene. There were a few items that needed to be talked about, but each time we had the conversations, we found ourselves in complete alignment. I think to most it would almost seem too perfect, but the connection was too much to ignore. So, on December 3, 2023, Tabby and I officially started dating and found ourselves on the fast track to so much more.

Being in a relationship with someone who's just as committed to personal growth and discovery as you are is like nothing else you will ever experience. It's like your growth as a couple goes into hyperdrive, and you start making huge strides in your individual journeys too. There is this whole new energy that comes from learning and growing together as a team, and the connections you build are on a whole different level. It quickly became apparent that our connections transcended the physical and emotional, leading us to explore that of the soul.

Soulmates can seem like a cliché term in the romantic realm, but this is a word we do not take lightly. In retrospect, it is unquestionable that our paths were on a crash course to this moment. There are intricacies in our human design alone that proved this connection to be inevitable. At a social level, so many people have told us they saw it coming from a mile away. To this we laugh about how it would have been nice for them to clue us in sooner, but we get that timing is everything. Our relationship has unfolded exactly as it was meant to, and it keeps evolving in the direction it is supposed to.

There is a saying that what you are seeking is also seeking you. What's really interesting to me, is that what I needed most came in a package I kept telling myself I didn't want. It's like there's some higher power out there that knows you better than you know yourself. I tell everyone that Tabby was the missing piece I never even knew I was searching for, but I'm beyond grateful that she's in my life now. This journey has taught me to trust the guidance I get. It was a lesson long learned, but in the end, it is a story of how this mister found his miss.

Dr. W. Garrett Goggans

Dr. W. Garrett Goggans is an esteemed mentor who helps his clients find their unique voice, craft a resonant and impactful narrative, and identify the perfect platforms to share their stories with confidence. Garrett's encouraging words serve as a catalyst for the breakthrough his clients need to experience so they can take steps toward their vision - whether that vision is to share their story in writing or deliver it verbally to small audiences or on the big stage.

Garrett's passion for storytelling developed as a result of his own transformation from teenage runaway and high school dropout who struggled with extreme social anxiety to a successful mentor, speaker, and International Best Selling Author. He offers additional leadership and encouragement through the local events he hosts that provide platforms for verbal storytelling, connection, and community engagement. Garrett is also the visionary behind the *Triumphant* anthology series and speaking events.

Garrett resides in Colorado with his partner and blended family and enjoys reading, investing in his personal development, and spending time with his loved ones.

Dr. W. Garrett Goggans
Mentor, Author, Speaker
https://linktr.ee/drgarrettgoggans

'Miss'chievous Adventures

in Retail

By Jaime Obertubbesing

J was just shy of 17 when I stepped into Stein Mart for the first time. It was 2003. My young, fresh-into-the-workforce mind saw a clothing store for old, uppity people and a paycheck to support my car payment. I didn't know at the time that I'd spend my next 17 years calling it home.

Our Assistant Manager, Donna, was very intimidating. She was calm and quiet–a woman of few words. She hired me, but for some reason, I felt like she didn't like me. Never mean, but she always seemed way too serious, and it felt like she didn't know how to smile–she had the worst RBF. Unfortunately, her area of expertise was in visual merchandising, so we ended up working closely more often than not.

Our home department floor pad included about 12 display vignettes that we would get to remerchandise as they sold down. This was my favorite part of the job, because it was complete creative freedom to make small, themed scenes, inspiring customers to buy home décor. Donna would give me pointers and let me do my own displays. One day, a child had evidently been playing with a small tree frog stuffed animal from the kid's department, as it had been left behind on one of the vignettes. I stuck it in the tree of my display and called Donna over to see my end result. I'm sure she was more amused with my excitement over this hilarious little addition than anything, but she actually smiled.

Months later, I was tasked with helping Donna clean the stockroom before inventory. I would have much rather been doing just about anything else, as I foresaw a long, awkward day ahead. To my surprise, we actually had some really meaningful conversation up on that second floor. I learned that Donna had quite the sarcastic and inappropriate sense of humor. I shared that I was nervous about going away to college, and something about her wise words helped me feel more at ease. Amidst the lamps on the dusty top shelf, that little green tree frog resurfaced. I giggled and threw it down at Donna. She set him in a display tree on our way out that day. From then on, each time one of us would redo a vignette, we would move him from tree to tree for the other to find.

In those quiet moments, little did I know Donna would teach me many valuable things over the years, about retail, life, and friendship. She would come out to celebrate my 21st birthday, support me when I had to help plan my dad's funeral, and sit through both my college graduations, several years apart. Back then, I couldn't have foreseen that when Stein Mart closed, she would be my hardest goodbye. And I never would have expected to be one of the close friendships to receive a personal phone call from Donna's family the night she unexpectedly passed away. But one of the most valuable lessons I will always keep with me is learning not to be so quick to judge a book by its cover.

As a typical teenager with no retail experience, I had a lot to learn about customer service. I remember being called to the front for a price check my first week there. Celine, the manager on duty, handed me a price tag with an item and asked for a price check. I was really confused, because she quite literally handed me the price. I had no idea what she wanted, but also didn't want to look like an idiot in front of the customers who were watching me. I looked back and forth between the tag and the item blankly. Celine later pulled me aside and talked to me about not going back to check that the item number was correct. They were making sure that the customer wasn't trying to rip us off by switching price tags on their return. Boy does it seem so simple looking back.

I grew a lot within my first two years at Stein Mart. I went away to college, working on weekends and holidays when I was home. I was eager to learn and the first one to volunteer to help in other areas throughout the store. I loved the challenge and variety of doing something new and different every day. By the time I decided to permanently come back to Colorado Springs for school, I was quickly promoted to Cashier Lead. And when the Home Department Manager position opened up the next year, I was chosen over a seasoned area manager because of my expertise and drive. That is when the retail adventures truly began.

People who have never worked retail are disillusioned about how much work it actually is—both physically and emotionally. Especially emotionally. As a young manager in a store with an average customer base in their 40's and 50's, I had to quickly develop credibility and a backbone. I will never forget this one male couple that would habitually come in and cause a scene. Their favorite method of madness was to bring in photocopied coupons and break their purchase into multiple transactions so they could use one on every...single...item. In fact, they did it so frequently, that I am partially convinced that they may be the sole reason for the company finally changing the verbiage to say, "One per customer, per day".

However, this particular day's scheme was moving the sale signs to accommodate their personal shopping needs. The much bulkier of the two (both in height and girth) would come in first and fill up his cart with home décor and bedding. Like clockwork, his counterpart would sneak in five minutes later and peruse the other side of the store. As the manager on duty, I was called to the front to deal with the unpleasant, belligerent screaming, because the "correct" price was not ringing up on their luxury pillows. This behavior intensified when I walked to the bedding and spun the sign back around to notate that it was the comforters on sale, not the pillows. I have never been more satisfied than when he demanded to speak to a manager. I got to say, "I *am* the manager." He huffed off with a look of disbelief—I'm not sure whether or not he was more disappointed that we were on to his ploy or that my 21-year-old self was not intimidated by his dramatic scene.

About ten years ago, there was this big deal made about people with service animals having the correct identification for their service dogs. Who showed up to come shopping with not one, but two, hyper, miniature greyhounds in matching service vests? They did. Of course, the bulky jerk made it a point to announce upon entry that his dogs were legit, and no one better question otherwise. No problem. Quite frankly, as I'm sure you could guess, no one cared to speak to this man any more than they already had to. I was quite amused running into them at the grocery store down the street doing the same thing to those poor cashiers. But this time I was able to make eye contact, roll my eyes, and reassure the employees that they had done nothing wrong. I think everyone should work retail for at least one day, so that they can understand how valuable it is to just be kind.

As a smaller retailer, we often had to do our own loss prevention. And it is amazing the great lengths people will go to shoplift. One woman actually filled out a job application and then filled up her purse with watches and jewelry. We'd been watching her closely, so it was Celine's brilliant idea to interview her on the spot. My friend Krysta and I waited around the corner for Celine to open the door. She intentionally asked us if we "had the time", as the thief sat nervously clutching her purse full of watches and fumbling over her words. Shortly after the "interview", this woman literally threw herself and her Bible down on the ground in the middle of our ladies' department, in a full-on loud prayer session, confessing her sin and claiming some sort of insanity. Needless to say, we got our watches back that night, along with a show.

It wasn't just the customers that provided ample entertainment. Sometimes it was the employees that said (or did) the darndest things. In 2013, the company decided to relocate our store to a prime location in an up-and-coming shopping center about two miles down the road. This meant we had to liquidate the current location. They shipped us a huge "Inventory Liquidation" banner that had to be hung from the roof, but neglected to send any rope, so we sent one of our cashiers to the store. This was our first mistake. He called from Home Depot, confused about the specifications of his assignment: 100 feet of sturdy rope to hang a banner. What seemed like hours later, he returned from down the street: mission complete. Celine and I gracefully climbed up the roof hatch ladder in our dresses, on a mission to get the job done. As if a 90-degree day in July wasn't hot enough, it felt like 110 as the sun beat down on that rocky, concrete roof. We were not tall enough to hang over the ledge and see, so we asked the cashier to stand down on the sidewalk and guide us to get it centered. This was our second mistake. "A little to the left---nooooope too much. A taaad to the right. Yep! Perfect. Wait—no, up a little...how perfect do you want it?" It is a true miracle that neither Celine nor myself jumped right over the ledge to both knock some sense into the cashier and put us out of our sweaty misery. The icing on the cake was when he handed us the receipt from Home Depot—clearly the most adequate choice for rope was the cut-by-the-foot selection, totaling $100. All we could do was laugh.

One year, when payroll was exceptionally tight, we were "volun-told" by a regional manager that a former employee had just moved to Colorado Springs, and we needed to hire her immediately. Not only did this seem quite odd, but we were already struggling to give hours to the people who both deserved them and were relying on them to survive. Nothing annoyed me more than how this came across. On top of this, our store manager hated any kind of confrontation, so of course, she didn't put up a fight.

When Selena arrived, she was very sarcastic and questioned literally everything and everyone—in a joking, yet very direct, way. It felt like she knew just how to push my buttons with her comments and drove me absolutely nuts. One day, someone suggested that maybe Selena was a spy sent to our store to report back to the Corporate office on our store manager. Somehow this seemed like a logical conclusion that we all hung on to for several weeks. Several years of friendship later, I told Selena this story and of course, even to this day, she finds it more than amusing. Timing is just everything.

In retail, I had many opportunities to learn the true meaning of being flexible. We had an unexpected power surge one morning that blew the breaker behind our store, right as a candidate was walking in for her interview. The store was going to be closed indefinitely, so I jokingly said, "Well, I can call you to reschedule, or we can do this in the dark." She must have really wanted that job, because, much to my surprise, she opted for the latter. I led her by flashlight to the back and up the pitch-black stairway to the office, where we got through about 75% of the interview before the lights flicked back on. At least I could check obscure interviews off my bucket list.

Speaking of interviews, Selena had a friend she was highly recommending for a position with us. We already knew we were going to hire her, but had to go through the motions of proper protocol. Being quite the prankster, Selena decided it would be best to have the management team create the most bizarre questions and tasks for her friend to complete. Celine was the obvious choice to conduct the interview, so we amused ourselves by picking out a suitable outfit from the sales floor for her to wear. Dolores arrived, and I ushered her into the office, where Celine sat, decked out in a gaudy gold velour tracksuit with an obnoxious sequin-bow headband, smacking her gum loudly. Selena and I climbed on top of Donna's desk in the adjoining office, popped the ceiling tiles open, and strained to hear the outcome of this ridiculous event.

As one would expect, the interview started out with a series of questions. "Tell me about yourself…" "What's your favorite pet?" "Hamburgers or hot dogs?" "Last, but not least, do you drive the speed limit?" I would love to know what was going through Dolores' mind at that time. Strangely, she didn't get up and leave. Then came the practical applications. First was the inkblot test. Dolores was asked to describe what she saw in the multicolored paint splatter I had sprayed on a piece of copy paper just an hour before. We stifled our giggles as Celine's dry, sarcastic response cut through, "Hmm. I see….Not quite what we were looking for. Moving on!" Our favorite task was selecting a bunch of random oversized products and setting a timer to see how many she could fit in our smallest sized shopping bag in 30 seconds. We all jumped when the fire engine alarm ringtone went off to signal that time was up. Years later, Dolores is still amazed that she managed to get all the items in there and in record time. I'll never forget the look on her face when she walked out of that office, and we came around the corner to tell her it was all a joke. What's more surprising is that she took the job and still remains friends with us to this day.

Unfortunately, for Dolores, this was not the last time we would laugh at her expense. I used the master lock key to pop open her locker, "steal" her keys, and place a mannequin in the backseat of her car. And when the store was relocating, Selena and I drove halfway across town, to her house, just to drop a shopping cart off in her front lawn in the middle of the night.

Colorado's erratic weather was also the cause of multiple adventures in management. One of the most memorable moments was opening our new location. Day ten of our two week set up, we walked in at 6 a.m. to the entire right side of the store submerged in an inch of water, with no sign of a leak to be found. Panic, stress, and a few choice words later, we discovered that the water from the previous day's rain storm had welled up along the edge of the building and seeped underneath, through the floor. Five days before the grand opening, we were setting up industrial sized fans instead of the truck loads of ladies clothing that was supposed to be occupying the space.

Sometimes that building seemed cursed. Or maybe it was me. I always seemed to be the manager on duty whenever there was a dramatic medical emergency. From a woman literally walking into the stop sign out front–with her face, to a coworker having the first grand mal seizure she'd had in 15 years, to a man slicing the tendons in both of his thumbs when he chose to sit on a tiny step stool that couldn't carry his weight...it was always me. However, this next one was a story for the books.

It was the first night of closing with a new manager in training. 6 p.m. Literally all other leadership had left for the day, not 30 minutes prior. Through the glass storefront I see these two older ladies approaching the entrance. They stepped onto the entryway mat, one gust of wind, and they were gone. All I could focus on was the blood splattered window panes as I ran to the entrance to see the ladies laying flat on the ground about ten feet to the left, the mat strewn beside them. Stunned with disbelief, I screamed for the cashier to call 911, as both women were bleeding profusely from their heads.

Describing the event to the paramedics was like a scene from a movie—it was like the wind had swept them up onto a literal magic carpet ride. The paramedics said we had witnessed a microburst, or a rare and powerful gust with similar strength to a tornado. Talk about sticker shock for our new manager, as we documented the event with these poor ladies. Amazingly, they were both in great spirits, laughing at the irony, as they held the ice to the wounds on their heads. They said they have been friends for over 50 years and have had many adventures together. For them, this was one for the books.

There were also a lot of fun memories inside those four walls. We loved to play pranks to lighten the mood. One time Celine told us about this strange experience she had with a lady dressed in a cloak and holding a lantern walking eerily around the local cemetery. Shortly after, I snuck Selena in the store early one morning and went back to my car to wait for Celine, since we were the opening managers. Meanwhile, Selena dressed in a hooded raincoat and carried around a lantern from our home décor area, popping around every corner as we walked to the back offices, trying to catch Celine's eye in the dark.

We had a mannequin head that made appearances throughout the store as well. Her name was MaryAnne. One time we used it to convince an associate that a customer was sleeping in the display bed and asked her to go wake them up. So, she did, tapping the "leg" of the customer as she tried to get her attention, "Ma'am...ma'am...excuse me, MA'AM!". Another time MaryAnne resurfaced as a messy guest that snuck into our blocked-off fitting room. The fitting room stalls had swinging doors cut out at the bottom, so we propped up the head and even set shoes below the bench. One of our associates was hemming and hawing about how appalled she was at the mess she saw spilling out from underneath. Not quite under her breath, she exclaimed, "What a PIG!", as she went to push the stall open. She caught the reflection of the mannequin head in the mirror and came running out, "Ohhh no no no! Oh my goodness! What have I done! I just called a lady a PIG!" The few of us in on the prank were crying so hard from laughing, she thought we were laughing at her! We only let it go on about ten minutes before telling poor Patricia it was all a set up.

But retail is not always fun and games. It is inconsistent hours, long days, and hard work. Some of the toughest physical and emotional moments of my life came from my Stein Mart days. We spent more time with each other inside those four walls than with our own families. But through the blood, sweat and tears, we still managed to create memories that have lasted far beyond our time there. Even on the toughest days, we found a reason to laugh and comfort in the bond and trust we created. And I find myself missing that place more than words could ever describe.

Stein Mart closed its doors in October 2020, as the last remaining stores finally caved to the popularity of online shopping and the aftermath of COVID-19. I had worked there one month shy of 17 years. Quite literally, half of my life. I took the day off from my teaching job and met Olga and Donna to lock up the building one last time. We sat in camping chairs as we waited for property management, and reminisced about all of the adventures we experienced together, trying to make light of the heartache we couldn't put into words.

Fast forward to now. Celine has been my sister by choice for the past 21 years. Selena's family has become a second to mine, when I never would have seen it coming. Donna and I kept in close contact until a brain aneurysm took her life two and a half years ago. I am so grateful for these relationships that have stretched far beyond those four walls.

Stein Mart raised me. I attribute a lot of who I am to the time I spent at that store. I learned a strong work ethic, how to be flexible, and the value of friendship. At 17 years old, what I didn't realize is how much that place would become a part of my identity. And even more so, that the people I met along the way would end up being those I couldn't live without.

But most importantly, I realized that you don't have to have a fancy job or expensive things to have an adventure. It's about making the most of what comes your way and finding the good in every situation.

Jaime Obertubbesing

Hi, I'm Jaime! My two cats, Sterling and Snowflake, and I live in Colorado Springs, where I have been teaching for the past ten years. I'm an elementary school teacher by day, retail manager by night, and up for any adventure in between!

I got into teaching because I love the energy, passion, and sense of wonder that children possess. There is something special about witnessing that spark in a child's eyes when a concept finally clicks. I also admire how children feel each moment and don't hold back. I've always wondered at what point we lose that innocence and become so self-aware, so I try to live life through a child's eyes—enjoying each moment for what it is and the memories that come along with them.

I am known for taking pictures of everything–capturing a moment is so incredibly valuable to me. I also enjoy creative writing. Consequently, it has always been a dream of mine to dip my toes in journalism and editing. One day, I would love to make a career out of that passion.

Despite my crazy schedule, I always make time for plenty of fun. I spend my weekends enjoying live music, dancing, soaking up the sunshine as much as possible, and hanging out with friends and family. To me, it never matters what I am doing–it is enjoying the company I'm sharing the experience with. And I'm always up for a new adventure. After all, life is too short to be anything but happy.

Slaying Snakes in the Cockpit

By Susan Kilrain

I was extremely nervous preparing for my first flight in the F-14 Tomcat. I was the first woman pilot to train in Fighter Squadron (VF) 101, the training squadron named the *Grim Reapers.* As if I wasn't under enough pressure, Captain Chuck "Cuddles" Wyatt chose to be my instructor and ride in the jet's back seat. He was the squadron's Commanding Officer.

We suited up and headed out in the rising sun to preflight the jet. There are no flight controls in the backseat of the Tomcat, so the CO was completely at the mercy of my flying skills. As we taxied to the active runway, I rehearsed the takeoff procedures in my head. Switching the radio channel to the tower, we were given clearance for takeoff. I quickly completed the takeoff checklist and taxied into position on the runway.

The engines roared to life. Pushing the throttles into after-burner, we accelerated from zero to 160 mph in about 10 seconds. After takeoff, we continued to accelerate as I raised the landing gear and flaps and headed out to the training area over the Atlantic Ocean. The power of the F-14 exceeded all the other jets I had flown. I was thrilled to once again head for the skies after completing the lengthy ground school and simulator phases of training.

Everything was going well, until it wasn't.

About 50 miles off the coast of Virginia, things started to go wrong. A quick scan showed a hot oil temperature on the right engine just before we got a warning light. Following emergency procedures, I shut that engine down to prevent a more serious problem. However, the hydraulic system on the engine did not cross over to the left engine as expected, so I quickly found myself down one engine and one hydraulic system. To make matters worse, the weather deteriorated, and the main attitude instrument, that tells a pilot if the wings are level and whether or not the aircraft is climbing or descending, failed. I now had to reference the little backup attitude gyro down by my right knee to keep the wings level. When a lot of things go wrong in an aircraft, pilots call it "snakes in the cockpit." I definitely had snakes in the cockpit that day. The challenge is to beat them down one at a time.

In aviation, especially during an emergency, pilots rely on the maxim: Aviate, navigate, communicate. It reminds pilots to compartmentalize and prioritize in high-stakes situations. The highest priority is to focus on keeping the aircraft safely in the air. The second is to navigate to the desired destination. Only then, do we communicate what's happening to air traffic control. I did what was required to keep flying, turned towards the airfield, declared an emergency, and informed the controllers of the issue and our intentions. We immediately headed back to the airfield and were given priority to land.

Due to the hydraulics failure, I had to lower the arresting hook (what Navy planes use to catch the wire when landing on an aircraft carrier) in order to stop on the runway. With everything going wrong, I could have easily panicked, but fortunately, I had been well-trained. I successfully caught the wire at the airfield and only then did my adrenaline kick in. My knees were knocking as I climbed down the ladder. In retrospect, the flight full of emergencies was the best thing that could have happened to me. I convinced the CO that I could fly the Tomcat, and he was more than happy to spread the word to all the instructors.

It was only a year before that Tomcat flight, in 1993, that the Secretary of State, Les Aspin, rescinded the policy that excluded women from combat aviation. At the time, I had already completed the Navy's Test Pilot School and was assigned to test a new training aircraft in Patuxent River, Maryland. With those restrictions lifted, the Navy selected me to be the first woman pilot to train to fly the F-14 Tomcat on the East Coast. I happily packed up and moved to Virginia Beach in January of 1994. About the same time, two women pilots had begun training in a West Coast F-14 training squadron.

The Tomcat was arguably the most "manly" of all fighter jets, flown by the most macho of all pilots. In the months prior to, and for several years following the repeal of the combat exclusion policy for women, many of the men exhibited open animosity towards female aviators. The main catalyst was the fall out after the annual Tailhook Convention in Las Vegas.

The Tailhook Convention provided an opportunity for the jet-aviation community to come together, learn about recent developments, and talk one-on-one with admirals. I attended twice: once in 1990 and again in 1991. The days during the convention were excellent—I met and learned from amazing aviator role models and heard the direction naval aviation was heading. At night, however, the aviators threw raucous parties, and their behavior towards women became aggressive. While they were obnoxious, the other women and I could pretty much ignore the rowdiness. At the 1990 convention, a male aviator said something inappropriate to me while grabbing my backside. I quickly brushed his hand away and stated, "I am a naval aviator, so don't ever touch me again!" He slithered off, and I never saw him again, nor did any other attendee disrespect me.

In 1991, the parties on the third floor of the convention hotel spiraled into something darker. On both Friday and Saturday nights, women exiting the third-floor elevator faced a sea of men arranged in what they named "the gauntlet." Each time a woman exited the elevator the men assaulted, groped, and yelled degrading comments at her as she struggled to hurry down the hallway. I chose to avoid the third floor and all the drunken debauchery on Friday and Saturday nights. But Paula Coughlin, a Navy helicopter pilot and aide to an admiral, got the worst of "the gauntlet." As she walked past, several men grabbed her and attempted to pull off her clothes. Coughlin, fearing she was about to be gang raped, escaped and locked herself in a side room.[1] She reported the incident to her boss, the admiral. When no one seemed to be reacting to the allegations in a timely manner, she went to the press. The story blew up from there. After Coughlin came forward, more women, both aviators and civilians, shared their stories from the convention, and the Naval Criminal Investigation Service (NCIS) launched an official inquiry.

DOD investigators concluded that 83 women were assaulted at the 1991 Tailhook Convention. Many male naval aviators were ultimately discharged from the military, and the convention was suspended for a few years. Secretary of Defense, Dick Cheney, fired the Secretary of the Navy, and several other leaders lost their jobs. The Navy paused all promotions until each candidate had been cleared of wrongdoing at the convention.

In the wake of Tailhook, a huge rift divided the women and men jet aviators. At the same time, the debate over repealing the

---

1

https://web.archive.org/web/20141031000428/http://www.nytimes.com/1994/10/04/us/tailhook-whistle-blower-recalls-attack.html?scp=1&sq=Navy%20rape%20gang%20vegas&st=csed

Combat Exclusion Policy imposed on women in the military raged in Washington, which led to more men lashing out at their female squadron mates. Angry about the investigations and punishments, some male pilots ramped up their unacceptable treatment of female aviators. I still recall one of my Test Pilot School classmates announcing to the class that he "really [felt] sorry for the woman who didn't get groped at Tailhook; she must be a real dog." Of course, he knew I was at the convention and had not been man-handled in any way.

In the years following the scandal, many women faced intense backlash, especially those who spoke out. Coughlin ended up quitting the Navy due to the retaliatory abuse she faced. Many male aviators blamed the women for the new higher scrutiny, promotions on pause, and challenges to their "old boys club" mode of operating. I became disillusioned about Test Pilot School being the best of the best. As the tension increased over time, I uncharacteristically considered throwing in the towel and resigning. Ultimately, I reminded myself why I was in the Navy in the first place and that my dream of becoming an astronaut was possible. I chose to keep my mouth shut, not make waves, and stay the course.

When the Navy gave women the right to fly in combat, the common opinion was that it was only to appease them for the events of the Tailhook Convention. Few aviators thought any woman had what it took to handle combat aviation, especially in the Tomcat. I knew this was the environment I was heading into at

Naval Air Station Oceana in Virginia Beach and I was determined to prove them wrong. Having graduated from Test Pilot School, completing the ground school portion of training was easy – it was just another airplane to me. I was very aware of the sexist undertones from some of the instructors and felt like I was under a microscope. I am convinced Captain Wyatt ordered all the instructors to treat me like any other student. In retrospect, I owe him my gratitude.

The women pilots on the West Coast weren't so lucky. They worked and flew in a hostile environment, not caused by enemies of the United States, but by fellow aviators in their own squadrons. Of the eight women pilots assigned to squadrons on the USS *Lincoln* aircraft carrier as it set sail from San Diego with the first contingent of women onboard, only four made it through the deployment. Lieutenant Kara Hultgreen, the first woman to fully qualify to fly the Tomcat in combat, suffered a catastrophic failure while attempting to land on the carrier. Her death further fueled the boiling disdain for women aviators on the ship. Lieutenant Carey Lohrenz had her wings revoked due to a poor carrier landing record. (She later fought that decision and regained her flying status.) Another pilot lost her flying status, and one transferred off the carrier at her request due to the hostile climate on board. The other four women pilots served on the USS *Lincoln*, including deployments to the Persian Gulf, but had to endure an even more sexist and divided culture than before.

After that first flight in the Tomcat, I no longer felt like I was under the microscope and was generally accepted in the squadron. I had slain the snakes, not only in the cockpit, but in a male dominated profession. I was scheduled to join the USS *Eisenhower* aircraft carrier in the Mediterranean Sea; however, I never got the opportunity. But, in December of 1994, NASA selected me to train as the second woman to pilot the space shuttle. I was breaking barriers and living my dreams coming true.

The Navy afforded me the opportunity to fly, prepared me for piloting the space shuttle, and taught me how to aviate, navigate, and communicate when life gets tough. This mantra should be applied to any high intensity situation. I am currently a partner in a venture group, New North Ventures. For us, the "aviate" is to keep our eye on the goal while we grow the company and keep it profitable. "Navigate" is determining the path we take to reach our goals. Once this is in place, we then "communicate" our intentions. Teaching my kids how to drive a car, I always stressed to "aviate"--that maintaining safe driving comes above all else, and not to worry about making wrong turns, missing exits, answering a friend's questions, or changing the channel on the radio.

I owe my success to the many wonderful mentors I had in the Navy, as well as working at Lockheed, stretching back to when I was a little girl. Societal barriers conditioned women to believe that they were limited in their greatness. But instead of just accepting that mentality, I pushed the boundaries, and it opened doors to opportunities I had only once dreamed were possible. With that in mind I've recently written a children's book, *An Unlikely Astronaut,* hoping to encourage kids to dream big and never give up. I want them to realize that with hard work and perseverance, they too can accomplish unlikely goals.

Susan Kilrain

"You can be anything you want to be."

Astronaut Susan is a motivational speaker, author, board member, and venture capital partner.

She is a veteran of two space shuttle flights and one of the only three women to ever pilot the shuttle. Her first mission to space was cut short due to a life-threatening systems failure, while her second mission lasted 16 days.

Susan is a graduate of the Naval Test Pilot School, and she has flown over 30 different types of aircraft for more than 3,000 flight hours. Most of her flight time was in the F-14 Tomcat, EA-6A Electric Intruder, and TA-4J Skyhawk.

Susan is from Augusta, GA and holds a master's degree in aerospace engineering from the Georgia Institute of Technology. She is married to retired Vice Admiral, Colin Kilrain, who was a Navy SEAL for 39 years. They have four children and reside in Virginia Beach, VA.

Life Through Basketball

By Mike Meyers

I was born Michael Roderick Meyers II on May 18, 1976 to Michael and Gloria Meyers in Takoma Park, MD. My father, Michael R. Meyers, worked as a garage attendant at the U.S. Capitol, and my mother as an administrative assistant for Congressman Wilbur Mills.

Life was challenging for my parents, as they worked hard to provide for me on the heels of a tumultuous Civil Rights era in the 1960's. My mother, the former Gloria Elizabeth Lewis, graduated from the historical black college, Oakwood University and my father from the historical black college, Howard University. They married in 1971 and for years tried to have children with no success. Finally, while my mother was in medical school, I was born as her first successful pregnancy in 1976. Two years later came my sister, then two more boys in the 1980's. Despite four miscarriages, my mother demonstrated her resiliency by always keeping her faith. My father was a Seventh Day Adventist Minister for over 36 years, and they were deeply religious people. They committed to Christianity early in their lives and made a point to raise each of their children under the guidelines of our church. I credit much of the success in my life to my parents. I could honestly say all of my attributes come from them. I thank God everyday that I had parents that loved me no matter what decisions I made or disagreements we had.

My father is a masterful organizer and powerful preacher. His ability to bring people together for a common good is unmatched with anything I have seen in my lifetime. He was able to accomplish things by bringing rivals together as friends and using political savvy to accomplish mutual goals. He was never afraid to resolve conflict but often used his skills to avoid it. Navigating church politics for over 36 years was the most brilliant display of effective leadership I have ever seen. I have watched military battalion commanders and leaders fail miserably, because they did not understand their formations and the dynamics that exist within them. Their inability to relate to culture, demographics, and even generational shifts all contribute to the challenges they face as leaders in today's ever changing world. A leader cannot simply check the block on adaptability. He must be visibly seen evolving with tangible measures of effectiveness. My father was able to accomplish his objectives, because his vision was forward thinking. He also realized that his vision and mission was bigger than himself. Leaders who think and embrace the philosophy of exalting themselves will often fail at the task of caring for people. When charged with responsibility, they look only to see the benefit for themselves rather than the positive outcomes for others. I learned from my father not to push other people down, but to instead reward those who are working in your corner. He said, "Son, never forget where you came from or the people who helped you get where you are."

My father's favorite TV shows are westerns. He is particularly fond of *1883* and will watch reruns of *Gunsmoke* daily. He was one of the first African American Pages from the state of California to serve at the U.S. Capitol and had the opportunity to meet Martin Luther King, Jr. and Thurgood Marshall. He is an amazing father, and I seek his counsel often in strategy for understanding people. He is as he says, "a humble, black, southern preacher doing God's will."

My mother is a winner in all things. I credit the successful culture, spirit, and philosophy that I have to her. She was born in Cleveland, Ohio in 1949, and at a young age, moved to Carlisle, Arkansas, where she went to segregated schools and was often discriminated against. The bathrooms and water fountains were set apart where she lived. She often begged her father to go to school before she was at an age where she would be allowed to attend. Like so many African American girls in the deep south, she experienced racism and was simply just trying to get by, without becoming a victim of violence. I am often amazed at how people of color today sometimes struggle to understand the challenges that existed in our past. The calculated and systematic revision of American history in our country should alarm people. My mother had to fight for everything she got academically. Fortunately, my grandfather, Willard Delano Lewis, was an educator. He made life for my mother easier by granting her access to books and education materials that her peers had. However, despite being the top student in her class, a post Brown vs Board of Topeka Kansas Supreme Court ruling prevented her from being valedictorian in 1968.

My mother wanted to be a doctor. She wouldn't sweat the small stuff, just continued to strive to be the best. It was never important for her to have that recognition publicly. As long as she knew she was performing in excellence, she just moved on to the next task. My parents' story could honestly be a Hollywood movie, filled with adventures, travel, and events of historic significance. They witnessed the impeachment of Richard Nixon, and my father was responsible for the detailing and maintenance of the vehicle of the Speaker of the House, Tip O'neill.

My own childhood was also one of amazing experiences. Growing up in the 1980's, I witnessed the era of Ronald Reagan, Star Wars, the Challenger Disaster, the fall of the Berlin Wall, the Los Angeles Olympics and of course, the Great rivalry of the Lakers vs Celtics. My life was filled with ups and downs, triumphs and reality, and I enjoyed every single moment of it. One of the worst and most trying times in my life was the death of my grandfather. He was a World War II veteran who passed away from cancer in 1993. This deeply affected my mother, and it was a very difficult time for our entire family. However, my parents remained strong and navigated our family through this tough period, with words of inspiration and by spending time with us at church and on trips.

One of the best moments in my childhood was the introduction of team sports into my life, at the age of 13. I met my first coach and the only coach that ever truly cared for my spiritual growth. His name is Chuck Faust, and he is still impacting the lives of youth. My mother was always a driving force for my success. She had me tested for ADHD and other learning challenges that were incredibly new to education. On the advice of an expert, she pulled me out of public school and sent me to Christ Community Christian School (CCCS) where I met friends for life. I was extremely blessed to be raised by two parents with diverse experiences to guide me into becoming the man I am today.

I joined the military and completed 23 years of service honorably. It was one of the best periods of my life. But, I went to war and came back differently, along with millions of Americans that experienced combat. Did you know that 22% of veterans suffer from post traumatic stress injuries? I label it an injury and not a disorder because my mind was injured. The term "disorder" feeds the universal stigma that you are weak if you seek assistance. The suicide rate among veterans is alarming. I have heard rates as low as 17 and as high as 26 people a *day,* taking their life. The rate is so alarming that I was compelled to act and do something. No loved one should be left with the unanswered question of "why" when it relates to suicide. I started a non-profit, The Military Basketball Association, to provide military communities an outlet through competitive team sports. We have successfully completed our 6th year of volunteer military. As the Founder and Commissioner of this organization, we use sports as a connective tool to prevent harmful behaviors and suicides. The Military Basketball Association is the premier platform for athletes to compete in the military while also maintaining their mental health, fitness, and resiliency.

Building this organization was not easy. We started in Colorado Springs with only 16 teams. We had very little funding and everything was out of pocket cost to coaches and athletes. We now have over 1000 athletes and over 50 teams in military communities around the world. In our most recent event, we had over 20 partners and sponsors, and our Men's Championship Game was broadcast live on CBS Sports Network, May 26th, 2024, live from Philadelphia, PA. In the past six years, we have had zero suicides, and that is something that I am proud of. In addition, in May of 2024, we completed the launch of the Women's Military Basketball Association (WMBA), and we are excited to feature a second year of competition. Basketball is an outlet for our military and veterans.

Life Though Basketball is a choice. We want people to always choose life, and we believe basketball is a means to be part of something bigger than yourself. If you are part of a team, you are part of a family. That family becomes your life. Family life means you never have to go through any experience alone. Life Through Basketball is the mantra we follow in the Military Basketball Association, as a family that sustains mental health, fitness, and resiliency. Basketball as an outlet sustained me as a child, saved me as an adult, and is now the means in which I can save others for the rest of my life. I may not be an "Everyday Girl", but I am certainly providing adventures for the everyday girls, guys, and anyone that wishes for a unique and fulfilling approach to resilience.

Mike Meyers

Mike Meyers serves as the current Commissioner of the Military Basketball Association. As a founder and volunteer head coach for over 20 years, Mike Meyers has been one of the leaders in the effort to support military basketball with a globally established volunteer association. He is a one of the pioneers to bring military basketball to the world as a tool to prevent harmful behaviors. He is a retired, 23 year Army combat veteran. He joined the Army in January of 2000 as an enlisted Soldier with the MOS of 75B10 (Human Resources Specialist) and then commissioned in 2005 from ROTC as a 2nd Lieutenant in the Quartermaster Corps. In 2006, Mike deployed to Iraq in support of Operation Iraqi Freedom during the Surge. He was medically evacuated in 2007 and uses basketball to stay resilient and build mental fitness. Mike has contributed over 15,000 hours of volunteer service in various communities and utilizes the military basketball platform as a method to provide active duty service members recreation while off duty.

In June of 2017, Mike Meyers and Angel Acevedo founded the Military Basketball Association (MBA) which was designed to provide volunteer basketball coaches and players an organization that seeks to promote the military athlete. The Association is governed by its Commissioner, Deputy Commissioner, Conference Commissioner, President of Basketball Operations, and Basketball Council. It has currently accepted 4 Major Military Basketball Conferences that make up a total of 44-50 volunteer varsity level programs.

Every year the MBA hosts its Playoffs/Finals. Teams qualify and compete to determine the best installation in Men's and Women's Military Basketball. The Finals has been an excellent volunteer opportunity for members of the community to interact and support military veterans from all services around the nation and world. The tournament has been a great opportunity to bring awareness to suicide prevention and Post Traumatic Stress Injury (PTSI) while military communities celebrate men and women in uniform.

'Miss'guided Career Paths

By Shalesa Aldrich

*I*f you're reading this story, it means I'm already dead...

Not in a literal sense of course. But to the woman I used to be. A woman who was scared, lost, and lacking. A woman who had gotten used to disappointment and "failure". A woman who was used to starting and then just giving up.

When I was little, I got an award during our annual swim team ceremony... "Most Excuses". It was cute and funny then, because I couldn't have been more than six years old. But as I grew up, that stuck with me and became less and less cute and funny.

Fast forward a loooot of years. I was a young mom with another on the way, working at a well known jewelry giant. I started off strong, and everyone saw my potential. I continued to work there for six years, where I achieved the President's Club status multiple times. I became an assistant manager, store manager, and finally, my impact on the store was so high, I was able to make my own schedule. I was a sales beast and I loved it...well, I loved being really, really good at something. But behind that, it was retail–hours away from the family, being sucked into cliques, gossip, and a super toxic environment. I'm ashamed to say I did let that consume me for a while, and I became what I was surrounded by.

I tried a lot of things along the way to try and get myself out of there... Mary Kay, Beach Body, Optavia–direct sales...all of them. But it never stuck. I kept starting and quitting. I got comfortable being uncomfortable (not in a good way). And the whole time I was making excuses for why it wasn't working for me. This is how I had learned to operate.

Finally, so much life had been sucked out of me in retail, that when I found out I had a third kiddo on the way, I decided to leave jewelry for good. I knew it was best for my family.

A little time went by, and in July of 2018, my family vacationed to Colorado Springs, Colorado– my vacation oasis from childhood. Something inside me started moving. Something was calling me. The last night of our trip, we ate out at P.F. Changs, and our server proceeded to tell us his journey to living here. He and his wife were both servers. They had moved here from none other than Fort Worth, Texas (where we were living) a few years before. They had three kids (same as us!!!) that they were homeschooling while making a life for themselves in their dream city. I knew meeting this guy was more than a coincidence.

I talked Kyle into moving our family over 700 miles away. And we did it in March of 2020!!! Were we crazy? I mean...yeah, a little at least.

I got a job with an industry leader in insurance. I had heard they only hire two percent of applicants, so I was feeling pretty desirable. Definitely a confidence booster! The licensing facilities were closed at this point thanks to COVID, so they put us on the front lines taking COVID service calls. Talk about work fatigue within the first six months. I left after about a year and a half and went to another leader doing outbound sales. This was a world I had never experienced before. We were taught how to "network", how to get active in social media with a purpose, and how to get new clients. I stayed with this company about a year as well, but the culture just wasn't right for me. Third time's a charm, right? I moved to a small agency closer to my home and more convenient for my kids' sake. I continued networking, met some really amazing women with their own businesses, AND I quit drinking alcohol.

A couple of months after this change, I experienced some really intense mental shifts. I started to realize where my journey had taken me so far, what I had learned along the way, and, more importantly, how much untapped potential I had brewing inside of me. Things began to sour at my current insurance gig, and I decided it was time to do something for me. I was going to start my own business from scratch. It was an idea my family and I had for several years, since our Fort Worth days, and it was time to make it a reality.

S'mormet was born. I didn't skip a beat. I continued networking, inserting myself into new groups and staying in the old ones that I loved. I worked my butt off, pretending to know exactly what I was doing. I tried new things. I tried scary things. I succeeded, I failed, I tried again, and I learned... but most importantly I never gave up. I worked when it was easy, hard, and everything in between.

Here we are over a year later. I meet more people than not that know me as the marshmallow lady. I have a renovated horse trailer, mobile s'mores bar, magazine feature, two podcast guest appearances, a YouTube channel appearance, and the beginning of my own new podcast under my belt. I couldn't be more proud. I'm evolving everyday into a new human—a healed and more complete version of myself than I've ever been.

The moral of the story? Don't mourn the death of the old you. Don't count your failures, don't let your past define your future, and most importantly... quit making excuses! You were made to do something great...GO DO IT!!

Shalesa Aldrich

Shalesa Aldrich is a dynamic entrepreneur featured in *Everyday Adventures.* Her contribution to the collection, inspired by her own journey, tells the story of navigating various careers before discovering her passion as an entrepreneur. Shalesa's narrative is a beacon of hope, encouraging readers not to settle for less than what makes them truly happy and emphasizing that they, alone, have the power to change their circumstances.

Hailing from a small town in Kansas, Shalesa transitioned from a southern lifestyle when she moved to Texas, met her husband, and started a family. Four years ago, she and her family uprooted once more, settling in Colorado. With over fifteen years of sales experience, Shalesa took a bold step by founding a mobile gourmet s'mores bar, S'mormet Gourmet S'mores. Her business, known for its homemade marshmallows in various flavors, allowed her to leave her job as a licensed insurance agent and embrace her entrepreneurial spirit.

A strong advocate for female entrepreneurs and small business owners, Shalesa is passionate about supporting and uplifting others. Her goal is to share her life stories to inspire positive change in the lives of those who listen.

For more about Shalesa and her endeavors, visit her website at http://smormet.co

Three Generations of Small Business Ownership

By Ashley Anderson

My story begins with my parents. I grew up in Western Nebraska, in a small town. My dad started his own masonry business when he was only 22 years old. From there, he expanded to all phases of construction. My mom played a major supporting role in his small business over the years, from bookkeeping to advertising and all other various administrative work. From a young age, I watched as my parents worked tirelessly. Their teamwork and unwavering commitment to quality left a lasting impression on me.

Inspired by my parents' work ethic and entrepreneurial spirit, I decided to follow in their footsteps and start my own business that focused on my passion for creating art and lasting memories. I was 27, and already working full time, but my daughter, Mattison, wanted to start dance and gymnastics. I wanted to be able to say yes to Matti's request for extracurricular activities, but they were not in a single mom's budget. I had to think outside the box. I started out small and simple – with a vinyl cutting machine and a dream.

I opened up M&M Custom Creations. At the time, that stood for "Mom & Matti." I offered custom vinyl shirts, decals, and signs. At first it was a challenge–I had a limited budget for the startup costs, had to learn how to use the software, and had to figure out tricks of the trade. A few years after starting my business, I met my husband, who is also passionate about being creative, and he started working with me.

I focused on custom vinyl work, sublimation and handwriting preservation. The most meaningful to me were the handwriting creations. When my dad passed away, I was looking for a way to feel close to him, and there isn't anything more unique than someone's handwriting. I used this idea over the years to help people preserve and transfer handwriting from their loved one's old cards & letters onto pillows, towels, decorative signs, and more. My husband, Jason, made wooden signs and acrylic crafts with his laser, and we often collaborated on projects.

We spent a lot of energy learning and improving so that we could provide quality products for our clients. It's taken several years to get where we are today, but it has been a growing side hustle. We now offer laser engraving, custom wood and acrylic signs, sublimation, balloon garlands, backdrops, and marquee letters. We really enjoy being able to express ourselves artistically, while at the same time, creating memories for our clients. It's a dream come true to be able to do what I love every day.

During the pandemic and the era of e-learning and school closures, our oldest daughter, Matti, was home a lot more often.

She witnessed firsthand how exciting running your own business can be and decided to start her own jewelry-making business, Made by Matti, at ten years old. Jason and I helped her make a Facebook page, which she initially used to sell her products door-to-door. She then expanded to booths at craft fairs, where she met other small business owners who invited her to have space in their storefronts.

Shortly after she turned 11, Matti was diagnosed with Type 1 diabetes. Now, she uses her business as a platform to spread awareness for the disease. She donates a lot of her jewelry to newly diagnosed patients, as well as other nonprofit organizations. She mostly creates unique earrings and necklaces. She has a line of jewelry called "It's Cool to be Kind," which she hopes will serve as a reminder to be kind to others, as well as yourself. Matti has now been in business for over three years and several local stores feature her creations. She and Jason also collaborate when they're able to; Jason cuts parts out on his laser that Matti then uses for her earrings and necklaces.

As for me, owning a business as a mom of three, while also being a military spouse, presents time management challenges. I've also learned to harness the power of social media marketing to help grow my customer base. And with custom work, there are often small problems that arise that require me to use my creative side to overcome. But looking back, I think my dad would be proud to know that he inspired his daughter and granddaughter to follow in his footsteps. The lessons I've learned running my own business and the qualities that he instilled in me, such as perseverance, all serve me well in many areas of my life, especially when life throws a curveball. However, at the end of the day, I hope that I can inspire my daughters (currently ages 13, 3, and 1) to always chase their dreams, even on the hard days.

Ashley Anderson

Hello, I'm Ashley! I live in Colorado Springs with my husband and three beautiful daughters, Matti, Maci, and Marlee. My husband Jason is retiring from the military after 21 years, and we've decided to stay in Colorado Springs! Two of our daughters are competitive dancers with Revolution Dance Academy. Matti, our oldest, is a youth advocate for the Children's Diabetes Foundation. Our family is very involved with both organizations. We appreciate being able to provide support and be involved as they pursue their passions.

I am currently on the board of directors for a local non-profit, the Rocky Mountain Dance Education Foundation. As a former dancer-turned-dance mom, I am super passionate about–keeping dance education attainable. This organization does this by providing scholarships, fundraising opportunities, classes and workshops, and our dancer relief fund. It has been such a positive resource for our local dance community, and I am proud to have been a part of it.

Outside of being a mom, I own Anderson Designs, LLC. We specialize in custom signs, balloon garlands, and marquee rentals. What originally started as a way to pay for dance, has turned into a creative outlet that allows me to help celebrate others, which is something I am passionate about.

We are in a very busy chapter of life with a teen and toddlers. We don't have a lot of down time, but when we do, we like to spend it together. We enjoy fishing, spending time outdoors, and camping! I just turned 35 and have a list of 40 things to do before I turn 40; we were recently able to check off a fun one–buying a camper! We are looking forward to making it our own and creating memories together!

Noble Cause Adventures

in the Workforce

By W.E.B. Claus
(William Edwin Baxter)

I was born with birth injuries in 1954, leaving me intellectually and developmentally disabled. Though these injuries didn't render me as one who was mentally challenged, they prevented me from performing multi-task work after I graduated from California State University East Bay in 1979. I was restricted to blue-collar or manual labor. However, God opened up the doors for jobs with single-task and low status work, for companies that served noble causes in the community, for mankind, and most importantly, for God's Kingdom. This is a story of some of the highlights of my work years where I got to support these companies.

In November of 1981, a couple years after graduating from college, a friend referred me to World Vision Inc., a Christian missionary organization in Monrovia, CA. I was hired as a mail handler to work in the printing and mailing department building, where I helped to send out bulk mailings to members throughout the United States. Despite long hours at times and working on the weekends, the job was right up my alley. More importantly, I was serving the mission of World Vision Inc. Even as a mail handler, I knew I had a hand in helping spread the Gospel and the love of Christ to troubled and impoverished areas throughout the world. It gave me great satisfaction in my work, despite the low status of the job. Of all the places I worked for, the printing and mailing department at World Vision Inc. was the workplace with the most high-jinks.

One afternoon, while I was operating the mail tier, which was used to tie bundles of mail with the same zip codes or the same states together, I accidentally punctured my finger with the "beak", which is the mechanism in the machine that ties the string and cuts it. I, of course, had to have stitches. The next day, a co-worker sketched a caricature of me as a hairy monster. With his sense of humor, he drew a cartoon of a monster bird of prey, complete with a bill shaped like the "beak" from the mail tier machine. He named the caricature, *Godbilla Versus the Beak Monster*.

Another day, the zipper in my pants completely busted. My solution was to cover the area with masking tape. However, the bright yellow was not much of a disguise for the broken zipper against my blue pants, which certainly got loads of laughs from my co-workers out on the floor. My supervisor immediately gave me something to tie around my waste to hide both the problem, and the obnoxious tape. And little did he know that many times when he wasn't looking, all of us in the entire printing and mailing department would engage in rubber band, paper wad, and rag-ball fights.

At World Vision Inc., Chapel Services were held every Wednesday morning. I became part of a men's quartet that sang special music during various chapel services. I was the baritone. One time, I sang a well-received solo during a chapel service. We had daily Bible devotions every morning when we didn't have chapel. Working with other believers in Christ and using my gift of singing were such blessings to me. I felt content despite the low status and low pay. My success in the workforce would always be measured by working for companies and organizations who served both noble causes in the community and God's Kingdom.

During the last few months, the company executives discovered that they would be able to send more money and resources overseas to people in need if the organization became entirely white collar. This would start outsourcing the blue collar work. In September of 1983, just shy of my 29th birthday, I was laid off. I resented that at first, but later realized that God now had another plan for my life. And I was only unemployed for a short time.

In October of 1983, I started working for Wycliffe Bible Translators, a missionary organization, based out of Huntington Beach California. People who worked for Wycliffe both in office and out in the field helped the organization spread the Gospel of Jesus Christ and translate the Holy Bible in remote places throughout the world. I had the privilege of working at the Huntington Beach Headquarters first as a receiving clerk and later in the bookroom. I had a serious accident while I was working as the receiving clerk. While a fellow worker and I were folding the lift gate back up under the company truck, it slipped out of our hands. The gate slammed down on my left foot, breaking four of my toes, and I had to have surgery to pin my foot back together again.

After the surgery, I was returned to my hospital room and served dinner while my co-workers were visiting me. Anesthesia used for surgery is known to make someone very nauseous. The dietician had made the colossal mistake of giving me a salad with green goddess dressing. One mouthful of that salad, and one of my coworkers was quickly yelling, "*NURSE!*" I was so out of it with the anesthesia, I was holding the bed-pan right up to my face and still managed to miss it completely. That was a real mess, to say the least.

While I was home recovering for several weeks, I learned that the company was going to get a forklift. They felt I should not operate it in light of my accident, so when I returned to work, I was transferred to the Wycliffe bookroom. The bookroom was more or less a warehouse for Wycliffe Books and Literature, so I got to fill mail and UPS orders and then package and ship them to people all over the country. Wycliffe also had chapel services twice a week, so once again, I often got to share my gift of vocal music. In the spring of 1985, a decision was made to make my job in the bookroom more of a sales position. My supervisor knew sales was not my cup of tea, so I was laid off in June of 1985, after a year and a half of service.

My next stop, a few months later, was working for Full Gospel Business Men's Fellowship International (FGBMFI), another Christian organization located in Costa Mesa, California in the 1980's. One of the noble causes for this organization was providing opportunities for businessmen to come together for prayer and Christian fellowship. In October 1985, I joined the FGBMFI team as a warehouse clerk. This was right up my alley as a single-task job, combining all the blue collar skills I learned from World Vision and Wycliffe, with an opportunity to learn more. Tasks included warehousing, light courier work, making daily company bank deposits at the Bank of America, preparing foreign mail and document shipments for Federal Express and DHL Worldwide. Just as my previous employers, FGBMFI had weekly chapel services too, so I was again able to showcase my musical gift of singing. One time in Chapel, I even got to share my Christian testimony, which turned out to be a blessing to a lot of people. FGBMFI puts out a monthly magazine publication entitled *VOICE Magazine*, which highlights inspiring Christian testimonies. Mine was transcribed in the September 1987 edition, where I became a published author for the first time just prior to my 33rd birthday. The title of my testimony was "There's Weirdo!", which would later be reprinted both in my book, *W.E.B. Tales* in May 2018 and another one of my children's books.

After leaving FGBMFI in 1991, I spent the 90's and most of the first decade after Y2K working jobs in the healthcare industry. The first few years, I was a medical courier and then moved to white collar multitask work from 1999 to 2007. This didn't work out too well for me with my disability. My best job during my work years was yet to come with Service Source Inc. out at Fort Carson, Colorado.

Moving to Colorado Springs in August 2010 to be closer to family was life changing. I finally discovered some family secrets that explained a lot about who I was. I learned that I was a forceps baby when I was born, which did extensive damage to my central nervous system and resulted in me being Intellectually/Developmentally Disabled (I/DD). Before that, I thought Tourette Syndrome was the extent of my problems. My family, particularly my mother, kept that a secret from me so that I could have a shot at as close to a normal life as possible. That gamble paid off, and gave me the edge I needed to get through life. As I was looking to retire on Social Security Disability my first year living in Colorado, I needed to know the truth about myself. In the Spring of 2012, I was diagnosed with Bipolar Disorder. I was now totally in touch with who and what I was, a man who is I/DD. My family found a social worker for me who helped me to get a job as a volunteer working at The Arc of the Pikes Peak Region (PPR) thrift store. The Arc PPR is an organization which helps people with I/DD. As a back-up plan to early retirement, the social worker helped me to sign up with the Colorado Department of Vocational Rehabilitation (DVR). This eventually put me on the road to working at Service Source Inc., the best job I ever held down.

I belong to a family tree of U.S Veterans and war heroes. There were times I felt that I missed out by not serving in any of the U.S. Armed Forces because of my disabilities. At times, I even wished I could have served as a Civilian Contract Worker on a military installation like my mother, Enid W. Baxter, did prior to WWII.

Turns out, Service Source Inc, in Colorado Springs, CO, was about to grant my wish. During the job interview, the rehab manager, John Wilson, saw how much I wanted this and hired me. As a Civilian Contract Worker, I was helping young U.S. Soldiers who were putting a lot on the line to preserve our freedom and democracy in America. For the next 10 years, I took great pride in helping the U.S. Military with this noble cause, which showed up in my work performance. On August 21, 2015 (Age 60), I received the President's Team Award for Service Excellence. As dedicated as I was towards working at Service Source, the company was dedicated to helping all of its employees with special needs and disabilities. I appeared on a local public T.V. show and radio show entitled *The Story Project* in May 2016. I shared my story of wanting nothing more than to enjoy an early retirement in Colorado Springs, until I learned of this opportunity to work as a Civilian Contract Worker on a U.S. Army Post. My story entitled, "Change of Heart" was later published in my book, *W.E.B. Tales*. I described how my desire for early retirement sprouted wings and flew away when I learned about Service Source. "Where in tar-nation did it go? It done flew out the window, that's where!" That line brought a lot of laughter from the podcast audience.

On July 9th, 2016 (Age 61), I suffered a massive pulmonary embolism which nearly ended my life. However, the doctors pulled me through. Just as I was about to get out of the Intensive Care Unit, I talked with the rehab manager at Service Source on the phone, and he told me that I had a job waiting for me after I got well. Most companies would not have let ANYONE come back after an ordeal like that. Almost a month later, I returned to working out at Fort Carson with accommodations. I made a good comeback, and on August 18, 2018, I was recognized as Employee of the Year.

I worked full time out at Fort Carson for a few more years, retiring with Social Security on my 66th birthday, October 11, 2020, towards the end of the COVID-19 pandemic. I had never worked for a company for ten years before, and I wanted to stay on part time for two more years, so that's what I did. I am now 69 and fully enjoying my retirement.

William Baxter

"W.E.B. Claus"

I'm William Baxter, but my pen name is W.E.B. Claus. I lived most of my life in the Anaheim/Orange County Area until moving to Colorado Springs, Colorado in 2010. There I worked ten years for Service Source Inc., which is an organization that hires people with disabilities as civilian contract workers in the U.S. Army Post at Fort Carson, CO. I am now retired and have become a published children's author and holiday recorded artist. I am also a season ticket holder for the Colorado Springs Switchbacks soccer team (USL) and have sung the National Anthem for them a few times.

I have been disabled from birth but have gone through life not letting this defeat me. Instead, I have constantly tried to go above and beyond my disabilities to accomplish great things and inspire a lot of people through my resilience.

The 'Miss'-Adventures of the Galapagos Hopper

by Kelly J. Calabrese

Roosters??? Yes, roosters! Well, I will get back to those pesky beings in a while. My adventure to the Galapagos Islands was like no other–communing with nature in its purest form, witnessing how Darwin's discoveries lead to new understandings of life on this planet. This beautiful and exotic trip was something I had dreamed of venturing for about 15 years. My wish finally came true for my 60th birthday. I went with an adventure group out of Georgia in August of 2023. There were 24 of us from all over the country, many of whom I had traveled with in the past.

The Galapagos Islands lie 600 miles off the coast of Ecuador in South America. The wildlife endemic found on these incredible islands are like no other on earth. We saw so many majestic creatures–the blue footed boobies with blue beaks and, of course, blue feet; the sea lions blending in so well, as they sunned themselves on the rocks; the curious penguins in their black and white skin, standing like statues on the rocks above and diving into the water, swimming so very fast that one even brushed against me. I stood in awe of the 100 (or more) year-old tortoises, extraordinary in their natural habitat, and the sea turtles and Galapagos baby sharks swimming eloquently through the water. I admired the Darwin Finches covering the trees, and the Cormorant pelicans and rare Frigate birds dancing in the sky. The Sally Lightfoot crabs were all clustered together on the rocks, the flamingos were breath-taking as they stood on one leg, and the marine iguanas were fascinating to watch. As for the enormous land iguanas–they were everywhere! At the airports, the boat ramps, the docks...they did not mind humans at all.

Transport in the Galapagos was like no other. Once our group arrived by commercial airlines, the real fun began. Ten seat, twin-prop planes flew the group from island to island. From there, mini buses, large kayaks, and a lot of walking were the main transport. During our stay, we visited several islands including Baltra (an inter-island connector), Bartolone, San Cristobal, Isabela, and Santa Cruz.

We traveled by yacht to the islands of Bartolone and San Cristobal, where we snorkeled and were mesmerized by all the land and sea life. It was thrilling to swim with sea turtles, penguins, sea lions, baby sharks, and a plethora of different kinds of fish. I love snorkeling, and have been an avid scuba diver for 40 years. There is so much to see underwater between the fish and coral reefs. The water is soothing and the wild life is incredible to watch.

The group visited Tortuga Bay, known for the best beach in Ecuador, as well as their magnificent sunsets. I am not sure why the beach was considered the best beach, but regardless, we had a blast swimming in the ocean and sitting at the beach bar drinking tropical margaritas.

The island of Isabela is where we ventured into the jungle for an incredible safari. We hiked up dormant volcanoes, explored wetland lagoons, and visited the giant tortoise-breeding center. Our stay was at the Scalesia Lodge, perched on the slopes of a volcano with spectacular views. We were set up in luxurious style tents, complete with hot showers, toilets, and very comfortable beds. Outside my tent was a very tall papaya tree with ripe fruit. I shook the tree to release the papaya...and it fell straight to the ground. *Splat!* So much for getting a fresh treat! But the view atop this dormant volcano was breathtaking. In the distance, I could see the ocean, but was not close enough to hear the waves crashing. And remember me mentioning the roosters? Well, this is where they come in. By nature, roosters are known to give a wakeup call around 6 a.m. Not these roosters. Their "cocka-doodle-doo" conversed at 2 a.m., 4 a.m., and yet again, at 6 a.m. To make matters worse, it was not just one rooster, but four! Those pesky roosters...who could get a good night's sleep???

On the island of Santa Cruz, the group explored the lava tunnels of natural volcanic formation, high growing endemic daisies, and the most elusive land birds of the Galapagos. We stayed at Finch Bay, a five-star resort with all the amenities. The only way to get to the resort was by dingy-water taxi and then about a five minute walk to the property. The food here was amazingly scrumptious, the rooms were spacious with very comfortable beds, and the pool and hot tub, delightful. Courtney, one of the 24 in our group, had a birthday during our stay. The pastry chef created the most magnificent cake. It was Grand Marnier flavored...delicious!

Santa Cruz is also where the group visited Charles Darwin Research Center. Darwin is known as the Father of Evolution based on the discoveries he made while in the Galapagos Islands in 1835. In fact, the islands are protected, and tourism is limited to preserve what Darwin acclaimed a couple centuries ago. Having the Darwin Observatory as part of our excursion was an extra bonus on our already wonderful and fulfilling adventure. Needless to say, our final days of the nine day excursion were wonderfully enjoyed by all.

Have you ever heard about Lonesome George? The Darwin Research Center was also once the home of the last remaining Pika Tortoise. I did not know about Lonesome George until our tour. Poor George could not find a mate, hence his infamous name. He tried to mate with many different tortoises, but it did not work out as they were not his same species. Poor George died alone in June 2012, at 90 years old, living only half of a Pika Tortoise's estimated lifespan. He was officially documented as one of the loneliest animals. How sad. Before visiting the center, I knew much about Darwin and his research, but I learned something new about this lonely tortoise.

My adventures in the Galapagos were extraordinary. It is difficult to say what the highlight was...swimming with baby sharks, witnessing blue footed birds, traveling in a 10 seater prop plane, walking on the beach or swimming in the ocean, sleeping on top of a volcano, or eating delicious cake. The trip was beyond any expectation I ever had. It was incredible to be in this exotic place that only exists off the coast of Ecuador.

"The love for all living creatures is the most noble attribute of man." -*Charles Darwin, Father of Evolution and Adaptation*

Kelly Calabrese

Hi, I am Kelly, and I have lived in Colorado Springs, Colorado for the past 29 years. I love to alpine and cross country ski, hike, dance and play tennis. I have 90 plants that keep me happy and a boyfriend that is kind, considerate, and a total hunk!

My professional career for the past 20 years has been in clinical nutrition. I help those wanting to get off their medications to live a vibrant and enthusiastic life through nutrient support systems and detox therapies. I practice what I preach, as I used these techniques to resolve my own health issues and wish everyone to have a happy, healthy existence, pain free, surgery free and disease free.

I earned my Masters Degree in Sports Medicine and Cardiac Rehabilitation from Indiana University and my medical and nutrition training from University of Colorado. I am the author of *Nutrition Diagnostics-Healing Through Empowerment* and may be reached through my website OptimalWellnessLLC.com.

I am grateful to be a part of this wonderful Everyday Adventure!

I Was a Stowaway in the Solomon Islands

By Bill Stanley

Stowaway - noun - one who is concealed in a hiding place aboard a vehicle as a means of obtaining transportation. Yep, that was me, but it wasn't my fault. Here's the story:

*I*t was a damp and airy night in Gizo. The rain had stopped. Bugs were descending with a vengeance unknown in the States. The *MV Iu Mi Nao,* pride of the Coral Seas fleet, was just arriving, five hours and one day late. I'm not sure what the MV stands for, but the boat's name sounded an awful lot like "You. Me. Now."

The place was the Solomon Islands in the Pacific, a little bit east of Papua New Guinea. Now called "the happy isles," these islands were actually the sites of some of the most vicious battles in World War II—recall Guadalcanal. Our objective, Phoebe and I, was to get to the Marovo Lagoon, a candidate for World Heritage status and reported to be one of the prettiest places anywhere.

We could have flown, but we chose to take the boat—big mistake.

I've traveled all over the world, but I don't make it a habit to recommend ships–and I strongly do not recommend the "You Me Now." Boarding the ship, my senses were instantly forced into full alert. The sights, the sounds, the smells–especially the smells–were overwhelming.

Hundreds of people were ascending, descending, transcending, and generally just milling around the ship. They all wanted to get either on or off the boat. And they moved all at the same time–everyone was constantly in everyone else's way. Line formation had not caught on yet in the Solomons. A jostle here, a jostle there–chaos reigned.

You can ask Phoebe about the smells–she has a nose for these things. Imagine, if you can, hundreds of Solomon Islanders at the end of a long, hot, humid, tropical day. Mix this with an equal amount of diesel oil and general mustiness, and then stir in totally rancid bathroom odors and you, like us, have arrived on board.

With backpacks on and determined looks upon our sweaty faces, we bulldozed our way up the ramp and steered to the nearest staircase, hoping to find First Class. We arrived to discover that we were not only foreign travelers in that section, but the only foreign people on the boat.

The room marked "First Class" was packed, filled with small, sleeping children covering all the floor space and draped across most of the chairs. It was air conditioned, as in the air was conditioned, but not cooled at all. It smelled terrible. Phoebe managed to find two seats next to one another. There was room either for us, or for our backpacks. We managed to cram into the seats and start contemplating the next 18 hours.

It was just about bedtime when we concluded that this just wouldn't work. Phoebe, who came up with this idea in the first place, calmly explained that we could leave the boat if I was unhappy. Just as calmly, I pointed out that we had left the dock ten minutes ago.

I had read in our trusty *Lonely Planet Travel Guide*, that the "You Me Now," had cabins. Leaving Phoebe to watch the gear, I searched for a crew member on the hunt for these hidden gems. Now this was no easy task, as the "You Me Now" crew had no uniforms and blended in with the rest of the passengers, most of whom were sprawled on one of the three decks.

I questioned a guy with a bullhorn who checked back and told me that all cabins were reserved. I later found out this too was just a passenger, but his information was correct: the only two cabins were taken.

Phoebe soon decided to take the matter in her own hands and see if she could better our situation. Off she went to find the boat's purser. It was then that the first of many ticket takers came by. There were, of course, no real ticket takers on the "You Me Now," just enterprising passengers, trying to reduce their own fare by helping the ship's crew. (Or could it be that they were really trying to take your money under false pretenses). I told the presumed employee that I had no ticket to take (true) and no money to buy a ticket (also true). That somehow satisfied him, and he moved on to the next.

Phoebe came back with the news that one cabin had been reserved, but the reservation holder hadn't made it on board. We could have the cabin once the purser could find the crew member with the only key. I was happy to discover that the pursers had as much trouble locating employees as I did.

Welcome to our cabin: a large window, a small porthole, and a lot of water damage. But, at least it was dry now. It also had its own bathroom, which smelled bad, but nothing compared to some of the other odors we had been blessed with on this ship. Best of all, there were two beds and two sets of sheets. The air conditioner even put out cool air! I was happy. Phoebe was seasick. But we both slept.

Then the rat ate our breakfast. Not content with taking just one of our bananas, Sir Rat took a nibble from all three. It wasn't so much that it was dark and that a rat was in the room that bothered us, it was the noise he made going through the plastic bag. It woke Phoebe, who then questioned the sound. Not wishing to be alarmist, I feigned ignorance as to the noise, considering this was a ship at sea.

With the next rustle, she whipped out the flashlight. I guessed it might be a small mouse looking for crumbs. That's when she saw it. I'm not sure who was more scared, the rat or me, but Phoebe's screams had the desired impact—the rat scurried right out of the cabin.

The next morning, I wandered around taking pictures of the many people blanketing the ship. I stopped by the ship's store, where I learned that the stock of edible bread had been depleted, and all the soft drinks with a recognizable name had been purchased. I bought a no-name, warm but fizzy beverage, and watched an entire deck of Solomon Islanders crowd around a golf game playing on the tiny TV.

Phoebe mostly stayed in the cabin, but at one point she did venture to the purser's office to buy our tickets. We traded a ticket back and forth when each of us wandered around the deck.

Finally, we arrived at Marovo Lagoon. 18 hours without food or drink was about to end. As I was sitting in the marketplace on dry land, eating some actual food, I looked closer at the "You Me Now" ticket—it only had Phoebe's name on it. I had officially been a stowaway on that ship. I asked, "What did you do?" She replied that the purser had asked for only one fare, so that's what she gave. "Besides," she shrugged, "The rat made me do it!"

Bill Stanley

"We've had an interesting life," said my wife on her deathbed. And that life has continued until this day. I am still working careers #6 (Financial Advisor/Money Coach), #7 (Author, *Money Sense for Young Professionals*), and #8 (Founder of a self-funded nonprofit, William Stanley Foundation).

As a money coach, I say your best investment is education, and your best education comes from traveling to countries with different cultures. I've visited 76 countries, but the Solomon Islands is one of my favorite places. Why? Because the people are so friendly. We were there in the 1990's.

Billy Butler is the pseudonym I used for these travel stories. I wrote them in an attempt to get published in newspaper travel sections. No luck, but many of my photos have graced the walls of coffee shops.

I believe that experiences are far more important than material things. I encourage one and all to write down things they have done, that no one else has. Me? I was a stowaway in the Solomon Islands. I've ridden a horse in Mongolia. What's on your list? I encourage everyone to focus on their legacy – your personal contribution to all mankind.

How High is TOO High?

By Sunnie LaMarre

*J*t all started innocently enough. It was the first time my boss invited me to come over after work and party with her and some of her friends. I was excited to be included in the "Cool Kids Club". I was looking forward to getting high with the boss lady and anticipated laughing our asses off. I got to her house before she did and used a key to let myself in. I had been there many times, so I made myself at home and went to the kitchen to see if there was anything I could do to help her get ready for friends to come over. I voiced a command to Alexa to play some 90's alternative music, as I was poking around the kitchen. Wine and snacks were already on the counter, and inside the fridge was a pitcher of sangria or something that looked very refreshing. I took two glasses out of the cupboard, set them on the counter, and poured myself one, thinking she would be home any minute. An hour later and a decent sized cocktail under my belt, she arrived. I poured her a drink and topped off my own as she pulled something out of the refrigerator for dinner. Shortly thereafter, her friends, Margo and Billy, arrived. Fresh drinks for everyone except for me, since I typically don't mix booze and weed, and I had been looking forward to smoking a little of her stuff. Mixing in the past has never ended well for me. But since sangria is little more than wine, I figured I would be just fine.

Boss lady invited us upstairs to her bedroom suite where we settled in to indulge in the smokable party favors. I looked down into the bowl of the small bong and saw something that didn't look familiar. She told me it was called "dab" and that it was just another form of THC. The container it came from read that it was 93% concentrated. The over-the-counter pot that I was accustomed to was in the 20% range, so the THC alarm bells should have gone off. Instead, I went with the flow and let the excitement replace any common sense I might have had. I thought I was in for a really good time with this potent stuff. I sat on the edge of her bed to have a toke. I mean, how high can you really get? It's just dope, for crying out loud. So, I took a hit and *whoosh*, a warmth rushed into my brain and coursed through my body. My eyes felt bigger, like they were cartoonish and bulging out of my head, as if to outwardly express how intense this first rush was. I felt amazing, like I could do anything. There was no pain, no anxiety, just pure happiness and the confidence that I could probably walk on water or leap over tall buildings at that exact moment, if I'd wanted to. I stuck with one hit as the others indulged in several. I thought I should wait on taking a second hit for a while until I could determine how this dab was going to affect me.

We were philosophizing about life, spirituality and wild experiences we've had. I was listening more than talking, as Margo was telling a story about a trippy meditation weekend she had taken a few weeks ago. She entered what she described as an "alternate reality" through breathwork and a dose of magic mushrooms, during this guided woodland retreat with her friends. She was telling us how transformed she was and how everything in life had changed for her since that experience. She was passionate, detailed and expressive. I listened in amazement and loved her ability to make me feel as though I was there in those woods with her. I was vibrating with happiness at this moment in time, feeling so connected and enchanted by each word. I was so undeniably absorbed, that I forgot to close my mouth when my jaw dropped the first time. Suddenly aware of this, I snapped it shut and hoped I didn't look like a fool sitting there with my mouth hanging open. Fixated on this utter lack of self awareness, I realized that I had totally lost the thread and forgotten what Margo's story was about.

As the gals moved toward the kitchen and mixed up another batch of cocktails, I went up to Billy, who had been listening to the story as well, and said, "Wow, that was amazing and super weird. My mind is blown". Although I couldn't recall the topic of conversation, I was confident the essence of it was still in my head and on the tip of my tongue. I just got distracted with the whole jaw-on-the-floor thing, and I needed a little reminder to bring it back to the forefront of my brain, so I could once again revel in the magic. I leaned over into Billy's personal space and said, "heyyawanasmokeoutisderwifme?" The slur brought forth a look of confusion from this guy and even I wondered what the hell had just come out of my mouth. He asked, "What did you say?" As clear as a bell, I repeated, "Do you want to go outside and have a smoke with me?" thinking I'd leave it to him to wonder if he had misheard me and that maybe it was him that was super high, not me. Then I remembered he hadn't smoked with us. Small detail. Moving on, I headed to the door and wondered if I could even walk through the house and out the front door without swerving all over the place and banging into something. But damn it, having a smoke right then and there seemed important, even if Billy didn't want to accompany me, so I went out alone. I was standing on the concrete, and it was cold AF out there. My teeth started chattering, but a little cold wasn't going to chase me away from this refreshing and quiet place to engage in my addiction. Plus, I was trying to remember in private what that super awesome and excellent conversation was all about. I sat down on the lounger and watched the stars come out as the mountains faded into the darkness.

As I was puffing away, reclined on the cushy lounger and lost in my thoughts, I heard shots ring out. I was pretty sure they were gunshots, but it was possible that I was imagining it. Regardless, living on the Northside of Minneapolis for a few years taught me that you hit the floor when you hear that sound. My smoke wasn't even a quarter done, and we were in Colorado Springs suburbia for God's sake...I was trying to decide if it was more important to lay there and finish it or to figure out how to grab my drink and belly crawl into the house to safety. When the second round of gunfire went off, I decided that I could do both. So, tucking my smoke into the corner of my mouth, I rolled off the chair and onto the cold concrete. I scooted to the door but couldn't figure out how to get it open without nailing myself. I threw caution to the wind and got to my knees, staying low. Grasping for the handle, I flung the outer screen door open, which promptly swung back hard and knocked the smoke out of my mouth, sending a flash of sparks to the ground. *Well that solved that problem.* You will have to trust me when I tell you that it is not easy getting your drink and yourself into a house with a closed door, on your knees, with smoke from your ever-loving cigarette streaming directly into your eye, all to avoid any stray bullets that may or may not be imagined.

When I got back into the house and up from the sprawled position I now found myself in, I saw everyone at the dining room table. Dinner was being served, and I took the last open seat. A plate of fish floating in sauce had been laid out for each of us. I sat down hoping that getting some food into my body would make me feel a bit less high and back in control. As I was trying to figure out how to get the fork to work to get some of the food into my pie hole, I started to feel tingly and weird. Dark shadows were coming forward. It seemed like someone had dimmed down the lights, and my torso was swaying back and forth. I reached for Billy's hand as he was seated to my right. *No wonder, I couldn't get the fork to work, it was in my left hand!* I got a little worried as the words fell from my mouth, "IthinkIamgoingtopassout." White spots were flickering on and off, and my vision was going dark. *Was I still outside? Why did it smell like fish?* I felt my face hit the plate and everyone rushed toward me. I opened my eyes and removed my head from my dinner plate with such a jerk that the saucy fish flung across the table. I had bits of fish stuck to my cheek and sauce in my hair. Someone was already on the phone calling 911.

The dispatcher wanted to know if I was conscious and breathing. I was. As the questions were coming and Margo was responding, I was getting nervous about what to say when the emergency responders showed up. I had forgotten that dab was a form of weed, and it had been purchased from a dispensary just down the street. It is highly concentrated THC and packs a wallop, and since getting high had been something done in the shadows for most of my life, I'd spaced that it's legal in Colorado. I thought I had to concoct a story that was elaborate and would keep us all safe from the fuzz. I mean, I had no idea who was showing up once that call was made. Even though I was stoned out of my gourd, I had some of my wits about me. I said, "Hey, you guys, you guys, come closer," as I started whispering, "We gotta get our story straight for when the cops show up. So what should we tell them? How about that I was running up and down the stairs and lost my breath? Or maybe that I was chasing that guy who was shooting outside and was going to make a citizen's arrest? Yeah, that sounds like I'm an upstanding citizen and doing something good for my community!" Margo leaned over and put her hand over the phone's mouthpiece and said, "The operator is still on the phone and it sounds like she's typing everything you say." I straightened up. *Oh crap, this is being recorded!* Boss lady joined the conversation with a noble idea, when she said, "Tell them that you smoked some weed and got too high." (Obviously there is a reason she's the boss.) Of course! It's legal here. "Yes, I'll tell the truth of course, I was just kidding around about that other stuff," I say loudly enough for the operator to hear. I took the phone ,and I told the lady on the line that I was okay, we would wait for them to arrive, and then hung up the phone.

While we awaited their arrival, Margo was climbing all over me, hugging me, rubbing me and holding my hands. *How can I politely ask her to back off and stop with the smothering physical contact?* I am not a touchy feely kind of person and this was way beyond my threshold of being touched by a friendly stranger. I tried to reclaim my personal space and said, "Look, if this is how it ends, I'm okay with that. I've had a really good life and my only regret is that I might drop dead at your party." Her eyes welled up with fluid, and she hugged me tighter. *Damn, that backfired! I should have thought that through better.*

When they came in the front door, I was seated on the L-shaped couch straight ahead. I was calm and composed, seated in a position that I thought would give them easy access to evaluate my situation and attach a blood pressure cuff, or whatever equipment they might deem necessary. Despite feeling lightheaded, embarrassed, and bad for ruining the party, I knew I was in a safe space.

There were seven professionals now standing in the living room looking me over. The paramedic sat on the couch to my right and the others formed a half circle around me. An EMT Nordic gladiator, wearing fireman pants and suspenders, was to my left. Next to the Nordic gladiator, who I decided to call Sven, there were two beautiful and strong female EMTs, a muscular and tall male

EMT, and two incredibly fit and smoking hot firefighters. The paramedic sitting near me was also quite attractive. His eyes were hypnotic, boring a hole through me, straight to my core. His face reminded me of silly-putty, and his intense staring made me squirm in my seat. I couldn't look at him directly as those observant and compassionate, yet slightly crazy, eyeballs were burning my flesh. I wanted so badly to reach out and move his nose around his face while squishing his cheeks. I planted my hands under my thighs to make sure I didn't violate him or his face.

As the blood pressure cuff was being attached to my arm, the questioning began. They asked, "Do you have any chronic conditions? What kind of medication are you on? Are you allergic to any medications?" I answered "no" to all. They continued with "How much water did you drink today? Are you dehydrated? What drugs did you take today? Have you consumed alcohol?" I said that I had hydrated, but probably not enough, and that I had smoked some pot earlier and had a drink. One of the lady paramedics asked in which order I'd done those things, so I admitted I'd had a drink first and then the pot. She recommended that the next time I indulge, I should smoke the pot first and then have the alcohol, not the other way around. *Darn it!* I knew this from experience but had somehow thrown reason and caution out the window this particular night. Having an EMT tell me the order in which I should imbibe in mind altering chemicals was something I never thought I would hear.

As the questions were coming from all the different medical personnel, Sven came up behind me and said that he was going to attach some electrodes to my back and chest, then hook me up to a machine that would take some readings about what was happening with my body. When the top of my shirt was being moved for easier access, I jumped and practically landed in Silly Putty's lap. Sven quickly backed off, and I asked him to let one of the ladies attach them. Everyone kind of looked at each other, and I realized that this was high maintenance behavior. I did not want to be that. In fact, I should be thrilled that this young man was about to stick his hand down my shirt! For crying out loud, nothing but stray bits of food had wandered down there in ages.

My thoughts were racing and going through scenarios that had nothing to do with the present situation, yet they came nonetheless. *Should I suck in my stomach? What bra do I have on? Is there fish down there?* Then the more rational thought: *For God's sake woman, these people are trying to make sure you aren't going to drop dead and seriously put a damper on the party, so get over yourself! This all started with a medical emergency, not a date.* I retracted my statement and said, "Yes, of course. Please and sorry." Three seconds later, the electrodes were on, and the machine was reading the results–another round with the blood pressure cuff and a little more staring by the paramedic.

Sven asked me, "Can you breathe deeply for us?" I said, "Yes, I am typically a very shallow breather, and I'm sure you were all aware of that. I'm sure you were saying to yourselves, *Wow, this lady is a shallow breather,* and since you are all eagle eye professionals, I wanted to let you know that breathing shallow is kind of my thing." One of the EMT's said, "Hmm, that is really interesting, so can you please show us how you can switch it up and take some deep breaths?" So I took some deep breaths as all seven of them watched. After a dozen or so repetitions, they seemed satisfied with my ability to do so. My blood pressure was taken yet again, but they still found it too low to end this surreal situation and be on their merry way.

I was finding it dreamlike and in fact, staggering to be in this situation which should have been very serious, yet I was somehow compelled to make it less awful for everyone. So I said, "Do you guys have a calendar—one with all of your photos on it that I could purchase in bulk?" To which they replied that they were thinking about doing one. I continued, "So did you all have to pass some kind of attractiveness test to get hired? Why are you all so damn good looking?" Then taking it further, "It is making it difficult to focus on why we are all here, when all I can think of is that you are all actors on some reality show, and I'm the one getting punked here." The smiles on their faces let me know that they knew I was speaking the truth—that they were all incredibly easy on the eyes and that this scene could totally be an actual T.V. show. I asked out loud again, "Am I getting punked? I mean seriously, how can this many good-looking people be here at one time, in this living room, attending to me, because I'm a little too high? Have I died, and am I on my way to heaven, for surely, this is what my heaven looks like." They all laughed and agreed that a reality show about them would be a success, and they had talked about it before. However, none of them confirmed that I wasn't being punked, so I held on to that suspicion for a while. Even though we called them, this whole scenario was still off the charts crazy-town in my mind.

The paramedic wanted to give me an IV for dehydration. I came up with every reason that I should not be stuck with a needle right then. They had been there for more than an hour at this point, and I was ready for them to leave. A call had come in over the radio attached to the paramedic talking about shots fired in the area, and I had to ask if that wasn't more important than giving me an IV. They said "Someone else is responding to that call, and our priority is getting you feeling better and your blood pressure up." They said that once I accepted the IV, they would pack up and leave. I just couldn't understand why all seven of them had to be there. I had run out of jokes and was annoyed with myself. But once again realizing that I was being difficult, I agreed to it. They gave me the IV, and I felt much better. My blood pressure was finally back to normal.

They packed up their stuff, and I walked them to the front door, thanking each and every one of them for their efforts and their help. As they were walking out, I asked if they got calls about people being too high very often. Sven replied, "We get them all the time. In fact, you were our third call today."

So, boys and girls, let this be a lesson–take care to smoke your weed before you drink so you can party like a big girl.

✦ Sunnie LaMarre ✦

Hello! My name is Sunnie. I hail from Minnesota–Lake Minnetonka to be more precise. I grew up fishing on a beautiful lake, where we left our doors unlocked and didn't wear helmets when riding our bikes.

I was fortunate enough to travel far and wide in my early years, and when I found myself at a boarding school in Steamboat Springs, Colorado, I developed a deep appreciation for nature and love of the mountains. I currently live in a treehouse with a breathtaking view of Pikes Peak located in Colorado Springs, with my cat, Happy.

My Bestie Pets

By Kay Rowe

hen I was around five years old, I wanted a pet I could call my own that would be my friend for life. My pets of choice, dogs and cats, were completely out of the question.

I coped as best I could, treating my frogs, turtles, and guppies with great care. I even entered the frogs and turtles in races at a lake beach. I took this rather seriously. So much so, that they inevitably became champions. As for the guppies, I saved several babies from being devoured by their dads.

My wish for a dog, a cat, or both, unfulfilled, I begged for one. My parents explained the magnitude of care, expense, and commitment required to have the pets I desired. My retort was that I was willing to pay the price, do extra chores, and help my brother more on his paper route, whatever it might take. The response was still, "no."

Then one day, a thunderstorm seemed to appear out of nowhere. My brother, sister and I were down the street when it hit. We raced home on our bikes, dumped them in the garage, and ran into the house.

Suddenly, there was a great scurry—a lamp and other items toppled to the floor. Then our eyes met. Before I knew it, I was pounced on and could not break free. My siblings were met with the same treatment.

What a joyous moment in our household! It was love at first lick. A beautiful dog (a cocker spaniel, toy collie mix) had been sent from the very heavens to live with us, or so we thought. We named him "Tippy," in honor of the way he'd presented himself to us, tipping things over in the flurry of his grand entrance.

Back to reality: My dad informed us that Tippy did not belong to us and had to be returned to his owner. He was allowed to stay with us overnight, due to the storm and it being so late. However, the next morning we were to seek out his real owner.

We dreaded getting up the next morning to perform the mission of returning him. But off we went, straight after breakfast, with my dad as our guide. Along the way, we argued that our mission was pointless since he was obviously a stray, having no tags, and not even a collar.

As we reached the corner, Tippy suddenly stopped and stared at a man who had just stepped out of his yard. First their eyes met; then the man looked at us, then back at Tippy. It was clear he was the owner. Still, Tippy did not move. Instead, he made a display of affection for us. We all cried at the thought of having to give him up.

Then the man walked up to my dad, and they shook hands. My dad explained how Tippy had come into our home during the storm and how we'd kept him overnight with the intention of finding his true owner the following morning.

He cut my dad short. "You keep him," he said. "I have never seen him so happy. I'm an old man, and what he needs is kids." Tippy understood every word, as evidenced by the licking frenzy that followed; first the old man, then my dad, then all of us kids. The deal was sealed, and we returned home with him.

Tippy was loyal to the extreme. He knew what we loved, and he protected us and our belongings – even our incubator chicks! One of our favorite pictures was of one of the chicks riding on his back. He extended his love and protection to my parents as well. We spent many happy years together.

I met my first bully in the fourth grade. That was minor compared to the seventh when the "I Hate Kay Club" paper was passed around every one of my classes for all to sign. Through these times, my saving grace was one loyal friend, Patti, and my cat, Mittens. Since this story is about pets, here are some tidbits about Mittens...

My mother and I had a long-standing agreement that if she were to have another child, it would be a girl. Quite frankly, I was sick of boys. It was difficult getting along with my older brother, and my two younger brothers were annoying.

When the day came for my mother to give birth, my father came home in the wee hours of the morning, peeked his head into my bedroom and proudly announced, "It's a boy! And his name is Richard!"

Imagine his shock when I screamed, pouted, and literally threw a fit. I told him, "Mom promised me a baby sister, and that's what I'm getting! Take him back! Trade him in!" Obviously, I didn't know a thing about the birds and the bees.

Amazingly enough, my parents teamed up and handled this beautifully. First, they told me he was born with a full head of long hair and was one of the most beautiful newborns ever. True, and I'm not being biased. They added that I was going to be a "big sister" to this little guy. In other words, I was going to be my mother's assistant in taking care of him.

My first assignment came quickly. Richard could not have been more than a few weeks old when my mother saw a mouse in the house. She brought us three older siblings together to resolve the matter. The solution? Borrow a cat from one of our friends. So we did, and the problem was solved overnight.

Not too long after that incident, the older three of us took a walk around the block to see our friend's six-week-old kittens. I couldn't resist; despite warnings from my siblings, I picked up a tortoiseshell kitten and we bonded. Of course, I brought her home, along with a plan on how to present her to my mother.

In essence, I said, "There's a chance there will be more mice, and we need to protect our little brother." To which my mom responded with a laugh, "That kitten is about the same size as a mouse. How will she protect him?"

I replied, "Don't you worry, I will take good care of her, and she will grow fast and be big and strong." Our mother agreed, and we named her "Mittens," because that's what her paws looked like, although they were not all the same color.

I kept my word, and Mittens was no doubt the most fascinating pet we ever had. She was part Siamese and/or Burmese, very loyal, smart, and a phenomenal hunter, as you will see from the anecdotes that follow.

When she was still a kitten, perhaps eight weeks old, I had to put her in the half-bathroom so we could finish dinner in peace. The only problem was that I didn't provide a litter box and forgot to let her back out when we had finished.

When I realized what I had done, I cautiously opened the door, not wanting to confront the mess she had probably made. To my surprise, she was standing on top of the toilet seat, her front paws stretched out and touching the toilet handle. She had pooped in the toilet and was trying to flush it!

One day, I was in my fourth-grade classroom when the teacher stopped the class and asked, "Whose kitten is that in the window?" I looked over, and there was Mittens with her face pressed against the window, staring straight at me. How she found the room where I was and got on top of that four-foot-high ledge, I will never know. I answered, "She's mine."

Soon after, it was recess time, and Mittens came right to the exit door to greet me. I gave her some water and told her to stay and wait for me and we would walk home together. She did just that.

She and I were kindred spirits. She slept with me every night, right on my chest. When I'd start to wake up, she would put her face up real close to mine and touch my eyelids very gently with a paw. She was fascinated with my eyes.

I remember a time when she was going wild in the house, growling and hissing, running to the front door, then the back, then to the front again, parting the curtains. I opened the door, and discovered that our bikes, which we had carelessly left outside, were being stolen. The three thieves were a house or so away. Mittens chased after them and pounced on the closest one's back. He dropped the bike, the others followed suit, and they all ran for it.

Another time, we were having a family gathering with Mittens hanging out with us in our backyard. Apparently, just for kicks, our neighbor put his German Shepherd over the fence. One would have expected a cat to run. Instead, Mittens stood there with her back arched. Just when the dog got close enough, she scratched him down the face, then she ran for it. They did several laps around our pool before finally, she ended up at the top of a telephone pole with a look that could kill.

I predicted there would be further incidents with this dog, and I was right. Two days later, upon coming home from church, we found Mittens chasing the German Shepherd on our front lawn. Then they ran laps around our car, so fast that we couldn't exit. Next thing I knew, Mittens was chasing the dog around the block. For the record, this block was about forty houses long. When she returned home, she rested on our porch, while the German Shepherd madly scratched at his owner's front door for refuge.

From that point onward, Mittens displayed a profound hate for all dogs. She even took to climbing up the tree on our front lawn at the sight of one, then pouncing from the overhanging branch, fifteen feet above the sidewalk, as soon as it was in her range. These anecdotes of Mittens are ones I still remember fondly.

When I got married in the early 80's, my husband and I moved into an apartment and adopted a kitten. We named her Roxy. Much like Mittens, she had unique qualities.

We didn't get Roxy spayed as we wanted her to have kittens at some point. When we weren't home, we'd leave a window in the dining area of our kitchen slightly open. One day when we came home, the window was wide open, and Roxy was nowhere to be found.

We walked outside and heard a cat howling on top of the roof of our two-story apartment complex. We looked up and saw that she was surrounded by eight to ten other cats. At that point, it was a sure bet that we'd be seeing kittens soon.

A couple of months later, Roxy jumped on top of me while I was asleep and proceeded to give birth to six kittens. I woke up in the middle of this and carefully scooted her over to the middle of the bed between me and my husband. We woke up to her nursing her babies and let them stay there for the time being.

As the kittens got older, she moved them, all by herself, into the living room. Then, after a scare with a male cat that got into the apartment, she moved them back to our bedroom, under our bed.

For the next move, she came out to the kitchen and literally grabbed my pant leg, so I would join her in the bedroom. Following her direction, I helped her carry all the kittens into our closet. She licked me, in appreciation, after each one I moved and then got back to nursing.

Many of the best days of my life were with my furry friends. They provided comfort during trying times. I can hardly imagine what my life would have been without them.

Kay Rowe

I am a peace-maker at heart. I live by the Golden Rule and am passionate about helping people enjoy a higher quality of life. I use my skill set to achieve this.

I am a freelance writer, author and writing consultant with 11 years of experience. I am also a licensed residential realtor in Nebraska and Colorado, as well as a mediator and mentor in the real estate industry.

I self-published my initial memoirs in October 2017 and more recently a redo of my memoirs, *Belonging-My Transformation to a Cult-Free Life*. The latter was accepted into the Library of Congress as well as my up and coming first fiction novel of a series, *Good Gawd! What a Mess!*

I enjoy an active social life in the company of family and friends, which includes social and business networking, music, nature, hiking, pickleball, and a myriad of other activities.

Driving to Alaska
Why the Dog had the Most Fun
By Cuzco the Dog

*I*t was Cuzco who enjoyed himself the most! Phoebe and I had an absolutely great time on our seven week, many-thousand mile, driving and camping trip to Alaska. We started in Northern California and covered the San Juan Islands in Washington, Victoria in British Columbia, the Alaska Marine and Alaska - Canada Highways, Dawson City in Yukon, the Canadian Rockies, and Glacier and Yellowstone National Parks. We generally had great weather, except for some rain and snow and mud. The scenery was magnificent—we saw deer, bear and eagle. It was a great trip! But let's hear from the guy who had the most fun.

Hi, my name is Cuzco. I'm a dog, and Billy and Phoebe are my human parents. I was ten months old when we started on this amazing vacation. It was radical, because I got to go in the car a whole lot—something that's usually just a 10 or 15 minute treat back home in San Jose, California. I met a lot of new people and even made some new canine friends. It was educational too, because I was surrounded by nature and got to walk on real snow and ice! The snow part is important, because I'm what they call a "mixed breed". My real mom is a German Shepherd, but we're not really sure about my dad. As a result of this trip, and my love of the snow, we now believe my dad was a husky. So the trip was sort of a return to my roots.

The best part was being with Mom and Dad just about 24 hours a day–something that doesn't happen all that often at home. And although there were a lot of hardships, it was better than any of the alternatives: being boarded at The Pet Place (cage and concrete), staying with the neighbor, Fred (who wouldn't let me do *anything*), or being visited once a day by Ms. Pet Sitter (boring).

My parents, Billy and Phoebe, did a lot of things to make the trip better for me. I rode in my kennel, sometimes called a crate, in the backseat of Dad's Infinity. This made me happy, because I like my kennel–it's familiar. I'm a den animal, and I feel comfortable in small spaces. I've been sleeping in my kennel since I was a little puppy. I could curl up with my old blanket, nylabone and two of my favorite toys, and no one could bother me. A big plus was the water bottle attached to the kennel door. It was one of those that drips water when you lick it. I spent a lot of time in the kennel, traveling and waiting, so it was reassuring to know that I had water whenever I wanted it.

I also had a supply of my very own food. Dad stored it in a big bag behind his seat. You never know what might be available in far away places or at what price. I don't like to switch foods, especially when there are other stressful things to worry about. I got to eat out of my very own bowl. I also got chew sticks, which I never get at home. They were delicious! But as the trip progressed, I began to understand that a chew stick also meant I was going to be left in the car for a while. Oh well, better to be in the car with a chew stick, then in the car without one.

In the beginning, I thought my name was B. Quiet, but now I know it's Cuzco. Besides being my name, Cuzco is a town in Peru, the ancient capital of the Incas. Pretty neat, huh? I know when I hear it along with "come" I'm supposed to go to my parents. But I'm young, and I don't always want to listen, so they brought leashes on our trip. There was the eight-foot leash and the extend-a-leash which reaches 16 feet! But when we camped, they'd tie me up to a tree with the 40-foot leash. I liked to wander around the campsite, particularly winding the leash around the tent guylines. Dad hated it though. Then there were the collars. My regular collar had my name and phone number on it—never can tell when I might get lost. My correction collar was for when I wasn't supposed to pull. (Now they know I'm half husky, and I'm supposed to pull.) And finally, the dreaded bark collar. I've learned not to bark when it's on; I've also learned I can bark all I want when it's not.

Since we traveled out of the state, I had to have my own travel papers. Before you travel, you should always have Mom or Dad check the rules of where you want to go. To get into Canada, I needed to have proof that I had my rabies shot. To get into Alaska, I also had to have papers that said I had been to the vet within 30 days and that I was "well." Only one person actually asked to see my papers, the nice lady who worked for the Alaska Marine Ferry. This pleased Mom, who spent a lot of money getting my papers in order before the trip. A couple of border guards also asked if we had papers, but never looked at them.

Crossing borders was still pretty neat. At first, the guards would ask, "What's in the cage?" First of all, I'm not a "what", I'm a "who." But I realized that if I just introduced myself, they wouldn't even have to ask. I just barked at them when they stuck their heads in the window, and they would ask, "Do you have any other animals?"

I liked riding in the car, especially if the day's journey was four hours or less. I could look out the front or side window of my crate or I could rest. Mostly I rested. Mom and Dad stopped every hour and a half or so and let me out. Good thing Mom had to stop frequently too. We had a ritual where they'd open the car door and the crate; I'd stand up and look both ways. I'd be especially happy if I saw green for grass or white for snow. Then I'd wait impatiently for them to put on my leash and say "release." I'd jump down, stretch, and check out the scenery. Dad would always have a little plastic "poo" bag for our walks. We tried to keep the environment clean, and it was fun seeing him fumble with leaves and twigs and things. My favorite words to hear were "go play", meaning that I could get off that leash.

Mom and Dad tried to let me run at least once each day. And run, I did, zooming as fast as I could from here, to there, and back again. Sometimes it was around our campsite. The best ones had streams and rivers to play in. Sometimes it was on trails near campsites or rest stops, and sometimes it was in the middle of deserted side roads. No matter what, it was still pretty fun, and I looked forward to it. I especially liked to eat the bubbles in the fast rushing streams. I usually was pretty good and came back to Mom and Dad when I got tired or when I saw my food dish.

I was always the leader on trails, charging ahead and then going back to make sure Mom and Dad were coming. But we had to be careful. Most state parks in the U.S. and Province parks in Canada have rules that dogs had to be on leash, and that included campsites too. In U.S. National Parks, dogs aren't even allowed on trails—we scare the wildlife, they say. Things were better in U.S. National Forests; I could go on the trails there. We just had to review the rules at each place and stay away from busy trails. There were also places with bear warnings. We took these things seriously and either stayed on leash or did not go at all. Good thing, because I know that if I were on a trail and saw a bear, I wouldn't be able to help myself. I would bark and annoy the bear, and it might decide to take corrective action. And I heard that bears can run 30 miles per hour! I'm not sure how fast I can run, but I didn't want to take any chances.

You really have to look out for all this wildlife in Alaska and Canada. I was sniffing one little doggie in Sitka, Alaska when I learned that his human mother had to watch him closely so the nearby eagles didn't swoop down and snatch him! Imagine, having to worry about eagles! And then there was the deer wandering around the campsite in Jasper National Park. I was doing my usual part to help Dad put up the tent by separating the plastic tent pegs, when I saw this deer near the bathroom. I barked to let him know I was there and scare him away. No deer allowed! This was a camp for people and pets! Well, he heard me, and instead of running in fright, he charged right over and was going to kick my you-know-what. Fortunately, Dad stepped between us and waved the rolled up sleeping bags at the advancing deer. I guess he saved me that day, and it sure gave me a different view of those nice Bambies. That guy was after me! So, from then on most of my animal viewing was done from the back of the car. A guy's gotta be careful.

Mostly we camped. I like camping because I get to be outside all the time. It worked out well because all campgrounds, private and government, permit us dogs. Several had restrooms that prohibited dogs inside, but occasionally, Mom and Dad brought me anyway. After all, what else could they do? They had to go, and I would bark if left alone. I remember once Mom took me in the stall with her, and I peeked under the divider at some other lady. Mom and the lady laughed. Hey, what's a guy to do?

I would sleep in my kennel in the tent between Mom and Dad. Sometimes, when I wasn't ready to go to bed, Dad would let me wander around inside the tent for a minute. I liked that. Then, I usually woke Dad up about 6 a.m., so we could go for a walk. I'd hang around on my 40 foot leash while he made coffee, and I became really good at finding old bones around the campsite. Mom always took them away from me–bummer. Most of the campsites had moss or deep grass. It was great. Except in a couple of places in Alaska, there were these little things called mosquitoes. My hair was long enough to protect me everywhere but my snout. Dad would put insect repellent on my ears; it seemed to work ok.

Occasionally, we would stop at a motel or cabin. We never had reservations; we just stopped when we were tired. Most places took pets, but you should check the AAA lodging books ahead of time. According to the book, one place charged $10 extra for dogs. I think Mom forgot to tell them, because I had to hustle in and out of the room. No problem, however. I'd be pretty good in the motel room. I had my kennel, and Mom would spread my mat on the floor.

I'd get pretty dirty camping, romping around outside, so one of the key things to take on a trip is plenty of towels. I'd get my feet wiped when I got back in the car, especially if I had been in the water or it had been raining. My kennel was on the car seat, but they covered it with a sheet. I had a couple of baths in motel bathtubs, which I hated, but after I got dry, I felt great. Mom said next time she will take some of this new dry shampoo with her. My bedding and towels would get really dirty though, so once a week we'd stop at a laundromat and do a "Cuzco load". I'd try to get everything dirty again as soon as possible. After all, a guy's supposed to be a bit dirty on a camping trip.

I decided I didn't like ferries unless we were on a real short trip. The Washington State Ferry system was fine because Mom and Dad could stay with me in the car or visit me any time during the trip. But I couldn't go upstairs with them; I could only go on the car deck. And I hated the car deck. Too many cars; too much noise. I much preferred to stay in my kennel in the car. Alaska Marine Highway Ferries were another story. Some Coast Guard law says that no passengers can visit the car deck while underway. But I didn't understand–I had to pay a one time fee of $10 for the Alaska trip, so that makes me a passenger. Why did I have to stay in the car the whole time we were sailing? And that was three, four, or even eight hours at a time. Whenever we stopped at a port, I could get off and take a walk, but those steel grates hurt my paws. Waiting for ferries was a bummer too, because you had to get there an hour or two in advance and stand in line with a bunch of campers. We'd walk around looking for grassy spots or near the asphalt. But I never had an accident. After a while, I sort of resolved myself to resting for long periods of time.

A couple of times we had to sleep in the car, because we arrived in the middle of the night and the camp site wasn't open yet. The first time this happened, Dad put my kennel outside and laid the seats down so he and Mom could sleep in the car. No way! I did my loudest, most annoying barking to let them know this was not acceptable. They figured out it was better to let me in the car with them. It was heaven. I got to sleep on top of them, all cozy and everything.

My meal times were pretty regular. I ate twice a day and really looked forward to it. No matter where we were or whatever we were doing, I'd get fed pretty much on time. Thanks Mom and Dad. My food disappeared in about 30 seconds. For reasons I will never understand, Mom and Dad take forever to eat, and they do it at least three times a day. It was best when they ate with me at the campsite. It was also alright when they sat outdoors, and I got to go along. But most of the time, they'd leave me in the car and disappear for an hour or so. But they were always very careful to leave the windows cracked so air would circulate, and I wouldn't get too hot. They made sure never to leave me in the car in the sun. One time in Alaska, when they went on a four-hour riverboat trip, they left the car key with the office. Someone came and moved the car a bit to keep the sun from shining on it. I could tell they loved dogs in Alaska.

This trip was amazing. Best were the new sights, sounds, and especially the smells—so much to smell. I really liked the snow and the glacier we walked on. Dad would throw snowballs and I would catch them in the air and eat the snow. Great fun! I met a ton of new animals—the cows, the deer (except that one that attacked me), the other dogs I played with, and particularly the ground squirrels that squeaked at me and drove me crazy. And lots of people came over to me on the trip. I find that people everywhere appreciate a good looking dog, such as myself.

I had a blast on this trip. But I also had to deal with lots of different and stressful situations. I guess my advice is not to use a vacation as a training ground for car trips. You need to be a dog who already knows both the inside of a car and the world away from home to handle all of this excitement. I loved all the attention I got from Mom and Dad, and it was great being a true part of the family. According to Dad, I grew up on this adventure. I left a puppy, and returned a dog. I am proud.

Cuzco, the Dog

Hi, I'm Cuzco. My mom is a German Shepherd, but I never really knew my real dad, so I spent my puppyhood identifying as a "mixed breed". The snow helped me discover that my dad was most likely a Husky. Boy is it nice to have some closure!

I love Nylabones, camping, and smelling new places. I hate being left alone, sleeping outside, and really mean deer. If I could spend all day off the leash, I would be in heaven. But, to be honest, I'm not always that good of a listener. There are just too many sights to see and smell!

I'm very helpful, especially when it comes to finding old bones, breaking in my blankets, and protecting my family. I've also been told a time or two that I'm a good looking canine. But I don't let it get to my head. In the end, all I want is to live a dog's best life, going camping whenever I want to, exploring all the new smells, and spending time with my wonderful parents, 24/7.

This is not where the adventures end. It's where they begin....

Join us in the fun! If you'd like to share your adventure, please scan here for more information on being a part of the next book.